FREUD AND EDUCATION

The concept of education—its dangers and promises and its illusions and revelations—threads throughout Sigmund Freud's body of work. This introductory volume by psychoanalytic authority Deborah Britzman explores key controversies of education through a Freudian approach. The book defines how fundamental Freudian concepts such as the psychical apparatus, the drives, the unconscious, the development of morality, and transference have changed throughout Freud's oeuvre. An ideal text for courses in education studies, human development, and curriculum studies, *Freud and Education* concludes with new Freudian-influenced approaches to the old dilemmas of educational research, theory, and practice.

Deborah P. Britzman is Distinguished Professor of Research at York University, Toronto, Canada.

Routledge Key Ideas in Education Series

Series Editors: Greg Dimitriadis and Bob Lingard

Freud and Education
Deborah P. Britzman

FREUD AND EDUCATION

DEBORAH P. BRITZMAN

Routledge
Taylor & Francis Group
NEW YORK AND LONDON

First published 2011
by Routledge
270 Madison Ave, New York, NY 10016

Simultaneously published in the UK
by Routledge
2 Park Square, Milton Park, Abingdon, Oxon OX14 4RN

Routledge is an imprint of the Taylor & Francis Group, an informa business

Typeset in Minion by
HWA Text and Data Management, London
Printed and bound in the United States of America on acid-paper by
Edwards Brothers Inc.

Library of Congress Cataloging-in-Publication Data
A catalog record for this book has been requested

ISBN 978-0-415-80225-3 (hbk)
ISBN 978-0-415-80226-0 (pbk)
ISBN 978-0-203-84150-1 (ebk)

CONTENTS

SERIES EDITORS' INTRODUCTION

This series introduces key people and topics and discusses their particular implications for the field of education. Written by the most prominent thinkers in the field, these "key ideas" are read through the series' authors' past and present work, with particular attention given to the ways in which these ideas can, do, and might impact theory, research, practice, and policy in education.

More specifically, these texts offer particular conversations with prominent authors, whose work has resonated across education and related fields. Books in this series read as conversations with authorities, whose thinking has helped constitute these ideas and their role in the field of education—yesterday, today, and tomorrow.

Much more than introductions alone, these short, virtuosic volumes look to shape ongoing discussions in the field of education by putting the field's contemporary luminaries in dialogue with its foundational figures and critical topics. From new students to senior scholars, these volumes will spark the imaginations of a range of readers thinking through key ideas and education.

1

FREUD, PSYCHOANALYSIS, AND EDUCATION

AN INTRODUCTION

> We do not pretend that an individual construction is anything
> more than a conjecture which awaits examination, confirmation,
> or rejection. We claim no authority for it, we require no direct
> agreement from the patient, nor do we argue with him if at first
> he denies it.
>
> —Sigmund Freud, "Constructions in Analysis"

Readers will have ideas about Sigmund Freud (1856–1939) and
his method of "the talking cure." You may know that the clinical
practice of psychoanalysis involves a psychoanalyst's meeting
with an analysand, or patient, many times each week with the
only request to "just speak" about anything. For this, there is
no preparation. The technique of "free association," indeed, the
idea of free speech and of being able to say what is on one's mind,
however, presents an obstacle to the analysand. Freud learned

that free association is affected with estranging thoughts: speaking them carries on the mind's capacity to associate things in the world with a history of anticipations and beliefs for them and calls upon the emotional fact of transference, that the wandering mind drifts through long ago relations and fixates, obsesses, and forgets them.

To look inside this odd beginning and to imagine Freud's psychoanalytic technique as allowing problems their fruition takes us into the heart of Freud's psychoanalysis and its novel theory of learning. It may also raise new questions as to what else happens within the contemporary wish for the proper technique to make conflicts of practice disappear. Freud's method of free association is otherwise; it plays in the field of objections and the unknown. Its other difficulties reside with the properties of language, so affected by the desire of the speaker and the other who listens. Freud added to this combustible mix the idea of psychical reality; ephemeral worlds of internal objects, agencies, fantasies, and trains of thoughts that, while simultaneous with external reality, do not coincide. In permitting this gap, psychoanalysis itself becomes more uncertain; the psychoanalyst invites what she or he does not know.

Freud took the side of this discarded content—obscure mental inventions such as dreams, slips of the tongue, bungled actions, fantasies, witticism, and forgotten memories—and greeted it as an objection to consciousness and as material to be narrated and interpreted. These curious affairs, for him, are the pathways to follow to understand the mind's astounding reach and its fault lines of vulnerability. Our nervous condition would instruct Freud. No wonder psychoanalysis is met with objections. Yet, more occurs. Freud would transform these objections into psychoanalytic objects—new vocabulary or constructions for analysis—that then would return as obstacles to psychoanalysis. All these narrative revolts compose a metapsychology of learning. They also characterize Freud's style of thinking, method of writing, and strategies of narration and teaching.

As for the talking cure, inevitably the analysand goes silent with the worry that she or he will run out of things to say, insult the analyst, say only unimportant things, feel his or her words as repeating him- or herself or, just as she or he steps into the room, decide not to speak and so have nothing to say at all. Ingeniously, Freud took all of this "nothing" as a portal to unconscious life and then as a clue that slowly gives way to a story of suffering. He listened to the patient's negations with curiosity and heard objections such as "That is not what I think" as signifying conflicts made from the deferral and resentments of representations. He admitted freely that the thing in itself, or the inadmissible force of experience, was ravaged by time and folded into revisions of new events. What remained from life's situations was the work of understanding the patient's style of apprehension and capacity for suffering. All this led Freud to treat speech symptomatically, erotically, and therapeutically: as both the florid scenery for the psychoanalytic act and as the patient's gradual means to transform an education she or he knows nothing about but that nonetheless influences the present with what could not have been understood in the past. It would be the patient's call.

Freud's psychoanalysis is a capacious theory of interpretation. His approach reads between the lines of congealed experience, reaching into the trouble with having language at all. One consequence of his interest with the breakdown of meaning is that he returned to science what at first seems an anathema to its focus: questions of affect, myth, and desire. When he presents his case studies to read like short stories, takes himself as his own best specimen, draws upon creative writers, and creates theory from children's toys to privilege the world of wishes and dreams, he moves science closer to the problems literature calls to mind. However, it also means that Freud would always be working experimentally against the tide of his own ambivalence, credibility, scientific education, and popular belief. Further, he admitted freely that his theories were beyond belief but felt that was no reason to abandon them.

Psychoanalytic audacity begins with fantasy life, dreams, and sexuality—passions that led Freud to what he called "the royal road to a knowledge of the unconscious activities of the mind" (1900b, p. 608). His early topics were commentaries on the vagaries and drifts of everyday life. By 1905, the novelties of psychoanalysis would be announced with a series of publications: the first book (1900a, b) on dream interpretation made from his self-analysis; another (1901) on the psychopathologies of everyday life; three essays (1905c) on sexuality; and one (1905b) on jokes and the unconscious. Over the next 34 years, he would continue to revise his theoretical and clinical foundations: dropping some ideas, reversing the order of others, heightening the problem of anxiety, and rethinking his own tendency toward certainty. More informally, Freud's vast correspondence would leave to others what to make from his misadventures, rough drafts, disappointments in friendship, and his persistent doubts. What remains constant is his patient style of listening. He heard words through the valence of their libidinal yearnings made from congealed, forgotten history and insisted that with the right kind of interpretation, the patient could think incredible experience through its narration, an after-meaning he called *constructions*, or a second chance to de-center the centripetal force of old events. Psychoanalytic treatment constitutes an apprenticeship in this fragile and fleeting learning, as does Freud's approach to writing about therapy and life.

His theories carried on with the idea that the subject of language is so ambiguous that its meandering meanings break apart with affect and so flee into psychical folds of the conscious, the pre-conscious, and the unconscious. In one sense, his views on language mirror the dream work, or the ways whereby dreams carry on their machinations through procedures of condensation, substitution, reversal into their opposites, consideration of representations, and displacement. Such motility plays havoc with conscious boundaries, everyday distinctions, and discrete categories. In another sense, language is treated as if it invoked only adjectives that point to the arts and crafts of infantile conflicts. He listened for the ordinary and extraordinary ways whereby individuals manage not to say what they want or how they say what is unmeant to say anything at all. That we are often speaking to someone already gone; that misalliances are unconsciously communicated; that the images and affects words accrue from our early lives cast a shadow on current terms of understanding; that the listener mishears what the speaker has uttered; and that one word can refer to so many things—all these transferences bring Freud to the rough edges of incredible and inaudible meaning, shards of history that compose and decompose psychical life. Conscious estrangement from these untimely events leads Freud to approach language itself as if it preserved and buried an archeological site; and, indeed, individual words are treated as relics, leftover fragments of experience that, when dusted off or pieced together with the difference of time, stand in for entire worlds of lost objects.

The analysis of dreams challenged Freud's method of listening to speech. He would sometimes take language apart and consult the etymology of a word to see how, in its use, an original meaning changes into its opposite or why a word such as *love* signifies so many events. At times, he will treat a word as a rebus puzzle. Words would then be taken apart syllable by syllable and also heard as garbles of sound, phonemes in search of meaning. Other times, words are received as puns, overflowing with the hilarity of affect that meaning barely conceals. Then, it can seem as though the unconscious is structured like a joke. Also, by thinking about words (representations) and things (presentations), Freud insists that words, like dreams, can neither exhaust their meanings nor be protected from the speaker's innuendo, double entendres, negations, or conflicts. The properties and structure of language itself have this rule of mutability: to hint, to disclaim, to deny, to hide, and even to shred intentions into unknown forms. These narrative revolts found in the nature of language, Freud argued, are also the working dynamics of human life. If language is ambiguous, it is only because it is a human creation that conveys more than it means and conceals more than is said. Putting things into words or refusing to do so, and saying the opposite of what one means to say, will provide one way to learn from psychical reality.

Yet the psychical events that compose and undo our emotional situation are as difficult to represent as their influence is to accept. After all, Freud insists the subject is unconscious and spends his life involved in the problem of conveying, transmitting, teaching, and learning from the dimensionality and dynamics of simultaneous experience and the frenzy of meanings discarded along the way. One receives a sense of Freud's original struggle in his "Five Lectures on Psychoanalysis," presented at Clark University in Worcester, Massachusetts during his first and only visit to the United States. Here is his conclusion for lecture two:

> You must forgive me if I have not succeeded in giving you a more clearly intelligible account of the basic positions adopted by the method of treatment that is now described as "psychoanalysis." The difficulties have not lain only in the novelty of the subject. The nature of incompatible wishes, which, in spite of repression, succeed in making their existence in the unconscious perceptible, and the subjective and constitutional determinants which must be present in anyone before a failure of repression can occur and a substitute or symptom be formed—on all this I shall have more light to throw in some of my later observations.

> (1910a, p. 28)

In its dethroning of consciousness, in imagining "his majesty the baby and the royal family" and "the primal scene," and by proposing the psychical as our excess and so as more than consciousness of it, psychoanalysis would reside in the dynamic world of objections, objects, and obstacles. It, too, becomes one of those "incompatible" ideas. Most of Freud's writing would begin from this other emotional fact, affecting the ways in which he transmitted his ideas and understood their reception. His last, unfinished paper, "Some Elementary Lessons in Psychoanalysis," returned to this founding problem, now as a lesson in resistance to psychoanalysis:

> It is not merely that much of what it has to say offends people's feelings. Almost as much difficulty is created by the fact that our science involves a number of hypotheses—it is hard to say whether they should be regarded as postulates or as products of our research—which are bound to seem very strange to ordinary modes of thought and which fundamentally contradict current views. But there is no help for it.
>
> (1940b, p. 282)

All told, Freud's psychoanalysis is incompatible with conscious meaning and invites both objections and a leap of faith that the inner world matters and holds significance in store. He will overturn meaning and de-center the subject. His psychoanalytic approach will be carried on through these objections and, in my reading of Freud, he will take objections so seriously that he will make from them psychoanalytic objects—terms of engagement—that will then prove to be obstacles to and the means for psychoanalysis. This paradox is constructed from the gut of human learning. My purpose is to introduce Freud's education on matters best described as unconscious and bring to the reader's consideration what happens, because of psychoanalysis, to the very thought of education and how we may give an analytic account of it.

The task of introducing Freud, however, comes with pedagogical dangers. Anna Freud's (1981) study guide to his work mentions two. First, upon reading Freud, there is a sense of estrangement for both student and instructor. Second, the instructor is apt to either simplify the material or render it too complicated:

> If the instructor wants to spare his student surprises and difficulties, he cannot help but falsify his material. If he wants to do justice to the facts, he runs the risk of demanding too much from his students and losing their interest and continuing attention. Freud himself strove throughout his life to take a middle course between these two dangers.
>
> (pp. 209–210)

This middle course, she thinks, is the condition for studying Freud. Near the end of her guide, she notes that Freud himself felt his contribution to the field of education as slight and that he left others to this work. In a short preface to August Aichhorn's educational text, *Wayward Youth*, Freud wrote,

> None of the applications of psycho-analysis has excited so much interest and aroused so many hopes, and none, consequently has attracted so many capable workers, as its use in the theory and practice of education ... My personal share in this application of psychoanalysis has been very slight.
>
> (1925d, p. 273)

Though Freud claimed little in the field of education, we notice how the idea of "education" casts a shadow over his work.

Freud did comment on mundane education from the side of its failure to communicate what the world is really like. He urged parents to discuss sexuality and answer the child's incredulous questions with frankness and impartiality. He wondered whether teachers could in fact prepare children for the harsh realities of the world and the aggression they would inevitably meet; wrote about the love of his teachers and their reminiscent authority; analyzed the frequency of examination dreams and the play of school in nocturnal affairs; and questioned what most affected his education. Further, he named "education" as one of the "impossible professions" through his consideration of the teacher's effort to influence others. All at once, the force of education expands to unimagined scenes and to what is unimaginable in the self. In any of its guises, education becomes our studio for human nature.

What psychoanalysis may mean to the contemporary field of education, however, does involve our estrangement, as it questions what we imagine when education comes to mind, from where these ideas come, and whether these thoughts can take flight with free association. Many people, upon learning about this book project, expressed surprise at the topic. They never imagined that Freud had much to say about education. Though they knew Freud explored the force of childhood within the life of the adult, most seemed to have a small, even parochial, idea of education, tied only to actual schools, to the good or bad curriculum, to the currency of children's need to be educated, and to their own experience of growing up. I began to wonder why education feels so timeless. Along with Freud, we will consider these objections as indicating childhood's relics and its buried wishes. Further, we shall call this return *wild education*, to bring into relief the status of the infantile: wishes for love, fears over its loss, and even, owing to the force of the Oedipal complex, the unconscious equation of learning and the need for punishment. What else occurs when adults enclose education within the fantasy of a child's being educated?

Perhaps the most difficult question Freud leaves to education concerns the relationship between learning and suffering first caught in the equation of learning and love with the need for punishment. Psychoanalysis began with Freud's self-analysis, undertaken during a time when he suffered, around the age of 40, a crisis of confidence in meaning and felt inhibited in his work. Two experiences of what analysis is like can be read in his letters to Wilhelm Fliess, some of which are published in the first volume of the "pre-history" of psychoanalysis, and give a sense of his struggles. On October 15, 1897, he wrote,

> To be completely honest with oneself is good practice. One single thought of general value has been revealed to me. I have found, in my own case, too, falling in love with the mother and jealousy of the father, and I now regard it as a universal event of early childhood ... If that is so, we can understand the riveting power of Oedipus Rex, in spite of all the objections raised by reason against its presupposition of destiny; and we can understand why the later 'dramas of destiny' were bound to fail so miserably. Our feelings rise against any arbitrary, individual compulsion ... . But the Greek legend seizes on a compulsion which everyone recognizes because he feels its existence within himself. Each member of the audience was once, in germ and in phantasy, just such an Oedipus, and each one recoils in horror from the dream-fulfillment here transplanted into reality, with the whole quota of repression which separates his infantile state from his present one.
>
> (1897a, p. 265)

Then, 2 weeks later:

> My analysis proceeds ... . Everything is still obscure, even the problems; but there is a comfortable feeling that one has only to rummage in one's own store-room to find, sooner or later, what one needs. The most difficult things are moods, which often completely hide reality from one.
>
> (1897b, p. 267)

Freud's own education was rooted in the *Haskalah* (the eighteenth-century Jewish Enlightenment movement in Europe), in methods of Jewish study of textual interpretation, in the promise of science, and in the Kantian Enlightenment dedicated to overturning superstitious thought and prejudices through secularity, cosmopolitanism, and the values of autonomy and thinking for oneself. He cared a great deal about literature, mythology, archeology, and science and advocated for the creative work of sublimation and knowing thyself. However, he was suspicious about education and its procedures and felt that certainty and unaccountable belief tended to wreck the creative work of thinking.

Freud has been considered as a moralist of the mind (Rieff, 1979), as positing what is most tragic about the human condition (Edmundson, 2007), as teaching a love of transience (von Unwerth, 2005), as inaugurating a century of testimony (Felman, 1992), and as creating new conditions for "narrative revolts" (Kristeva, 2000). That he is a creature of his history is not in dispute; there remains a body of contemporary literature in psychoanalysis and feminism that rethinks his writing on femininity and masculinity and proposes his masculine bias (Kofman, 1985).

Surely there is a great deal to argue over. More difficult to understand, however, is Freud's view of universality that emerges from the emotional fact of life: from the beginning, the human is a creature in love. The insistence is that for the susceptible, erotic human, constructing the formative past involves memory with its own intimate crisis of representation, an emotional situation that is, more often than not, forgotten and repressed. His notion of history is conceptualized through its deferred action and tied to the return of the repressed and the compulsion to repeat. Memory then is ordered and disordered by mythic time and is in conflict with something that is not history at all, namely, the unconscious. With these constructions, Freud defined the dynamic unconscious: an area of mental life that escapes time, negations, and contradictions. It urges the logic of the wish. This new affected subject, he argued, rewrites what becomes of "wild education" and what education can become.

Though Freud tried to separate the education of children from the work of psychoanalysis even as he oversaw the beginnings of child psychoanalysis in the early twentieth century, he considered psychoanalytic treatment for adults as an "after-education," dedicated to the work of self-knowledge. Constructions in analysis may be defined paradoxically as a means to think about what could not be known but nonetheless impresses unconscious life. They are commentary on and destruction of infantile pulls toward authority, compliance, and modes of psychological compromise best thought of as neurosis. In this sense, the idea of education that most influenced Freud was that of the Germanic *Bildung*, literary narratives of learning dedicated to reflecting on our nervous condition and made to link the disparate elements of culture and life to self-formation. Illness was Freud's implicit guide and perhaps a moral ideal for approaching the education of the psychoanalyst and the after-education of the analysand. A curiosity toward suffering and its destiny steered his many critiques on society and violence in his time.

Freud's pedagogical style stayed close to the pleasures and dangers of considering the mind's depths and disadvantages; the writing itself is a commentary on psychoanalytic constructions and his own objections to them. One can say that to write of psychoanalysis is to write psychoanalytically: to attend to constructions as transpositions of impression, reception, and use. A creative, lively, and often humorous example of this style can be found in his essay on the defense of the lay analyst, a non-medical practitioner of psychoanalysis. It carries the title "The Question of Lay Analysis: Conversations with an Impartial Person" and is written as a dialogue with the flavor and flummox of an argument. He seems to capture both the instructor and the student's frustrations in learning. There is the drama of an incredulous, inquisitive character that must ask impossible, maddening questions. Also, readers may wonder who is actually impartial. Freud admits that the analyst has only words. "But is it confession?" the impartial person asks. And then:

> We must reply: "Yes and no!" Confession no doubt plays a part in analysis—as an introduction to it, we might say. But it is very far from constituting the essence of analysis or from explaining its effects. In Confession the sinner tells what he knows; in analysis the neurotic has to tell more. Nor have we heard that Confession has ever developed enough power to get rid of actual pathological symptoms.
>
> "Then, after all, I do not understand," comes the rejoinder. "What can you possibly mean by 'telling more than he knows'"?
>
> (1926b, p. 189)

Negations aside, this little gem takes on every objection to psychoanalysis, which begins with learning that the rejoinder, "I do not understand," tells more than the objector consciously knows. Further, Freud (1927b) tells his readers in a postscript that he wrote this essay in defense of the lay analyst Theodor Reik, charged with quackery and taken to the Vienna Courts. Even as the charges were dropped, his essay does away with the consolation of agreement.

His style of handling objections began in his first book, *The Interpretation of Dreams*, taken through eight editions. His preface to the sixth edition, 21 years later, defined his writing task: "If its earlier function was to offer some information on the nature of dreams, now it has the no less important duty of dealing with the obstinate misunderstandings to which that information is subject" (1900a, pp. xxix–xxx). Misunderstandings—Freud called them "resistances"—were common. Correcting them was endless and done with humor, such as in his short anonymous article, "A note on the prehistory of the technique of analysis," wherein he admitted his method of free association was hardly original. The method was derived, he said, from a book he received in his youth written by one Ludwig Börne and carrying the title, *The Art of Becoming an Original Writer in Three Days*. The advice was to write everything down in one's head. In that note, Freud also drew attention to the problem with the method. Even if one could say everything, "too great resistances made the suspected connection unrecognizable" (1920b, p. 264). Why misunderstanding is so obstinate would be his most endearing topic.

Making connections between disparate experiences in the mind and so considering why thoughts cannot add up and what one thought has to do with another became the grand problem. Interpretation would construct these objects, obstacles, and objections to learning. By the end of Freud's work, there remains the question of how change occurs in the life of the mind and what sense could be made from elemental attributes of life or the relation between constitutional factors and accidents. So he invites his readers into more difficulties: "Instead of an enquiry into how a cure by analysis comes about (a matter which I think has been sufficiently elucidated) the question should be asked of what are the obstacles that stand in the way of such a cure" (1937a, p. 221). Such a study, Freud argued, would take one to the limits of current knowledge and also open unforeseen questions.

As for the application of psychoanalysis to the problem of human sociality and political life, Freud saw in these cultural processes memory problems of education, thereby stretching the concept of education to the mismatch of how the world is disclosed, received, and psychologically ingested. And this approach challenges what application can mean. He made education his construction site, presenting its inheritance as relics buried yet preserved in archeological ruins, themselves revenants of a prehistory of natality and its utter helplessness and dependency. Education thus became associated with unsolved problems of learning, as emerging from the unconscious, sexuality, and the drives; as susceptible to ignorance and memory; and as caught in the dynamics of love. This last link of education with love brings techniques and practices beyond their plans for others and into our psychology. Our topic, then, concerns how, with Freud's conception of love and estrangement, human learning unfolds and leaves in its wake development from the inside.

Selecting aspects of Freud's work with a focus on myriad forms of education means that I have had to place a great deal of Freud's writing in parentheses; readers will find the study limits are my own. The problem is not only the sheer volume of Freud's work, his wide-ranging topics, and his continual revisions. Freud authored more than 250 articles, notes, and books. A separate literature is contained in his vast correspondence with friends, followers, and major figures in science and the arts. I quote from the 23 volumes in English known as *The Standard Edition of the Complete Psychological Works of Sigmund Freud (1886–1939)*. These volumes were complied and translated from the German by James Strachey, in collaboration with Anna Freud and assisted by Alix Strachey and Alan Tyson. They were published between 1953 and 1964 and, in 1974, came a separate volume of indexes and bibliography, compiled by Angela Richards. Each article carries a short introduction by the editors that overviews key ideas, comments on translation difficulties, and notes Freud's ongoing revisions.

Along with this problem of sheer volume, however, a more existential one concerns the writer's desire and decisions as to what to emphasize and what to set aside. My working rule has been to focus on Freud's evolving views of the psyche as an open speculation on new ways to narrate learning beyond the measures of success and failure, themselves only an indication of splitting into good and bad. Freud's narrative style is thus interpreted as a way to create new educational accounts. Psychoanalysis is a means for linking learning and education to the formative past of infancy and the libidinal work of having to grow up. My challenge is to introduce some psychical consequences from the fact that any education is an emotional situation and that learning is a testimony to the fragility and enthusiasm of its own events.

Contemporary discussions on Freud benefit from the hindsight of being able to trace the history of psychoanalysis with the currency of Freud's vast archive of published letters, memoirs from those who were analyzed by Freud and worked with him, and splendid historiography on Freud's writing (Grubrich-Simitis, 1996; Greenberg, 1997). The secondary commentary on Freud's life, beginning with Ernst Jones's three volume biography (1972, 1974) and Peter Gay's life study (1988), and now the wide-ranging arguments in contemporary psychoanalysis and post-Freudian thought add further complexity and contention to the Freudian field. And his influence on popular culture—the ways in which films, novels, music, and art, for instance, can now be conceived and interpreted—suggests that if we are not yet done with Freud, it is because we cannot be done with affecting our own private scenery.

The Freudian field now contains competing translations of Freud's work, a number of introductory guides to Freud, significant historical and social studies, new biographies, new schools of psychoanalytic thought, and contentious debates on Freud's relevancy today. There are both Freudian slips and Freud wars. Contemporary psychoanalysis takes liberty in rethinking Freud's theories, yet also manages to repeat the deep conflicts and estrangements psychoanalysis itself provokes. I have kept these discussions in mind but do not venture into their controversies and insistences; nor do I comment on the development of other psychoanalytic thinkers—those within Freud's circle and the ones who come after—and what they have made from Freud's work. Indeed, Freud's work is always under construction. I have taken my lead from reading Freud and imagining pedagogical conflicts he faced as he went about his work and presented his ideas. In this sense, and as within any education, the great problem that preoccupies this present study is transmission, a style of conveying surprising ideas that attends to the problem of their construction, reception, and interpretation. I read the Freudian archive as an unfinished pedagogical project, as anticipating its reception, as affected by its own theories, and as progressively caught up in the dynamics constructed. This last problem of the transference within theory is one of the great dilemmas Freud leaves to pedagogy. In essence, pedagogy becomes influenced by what is unknown and 'paradoxically'; its work represents the qualities of its own ignorance.

Then and now, the Freudian Field is expansive and contentious. It cannot be otherwise, given that psychoanalysis is first and foremost a theory of affected conflict. This dynamic play of ideas, motives, arguments, objections, and constructions composes Freud's epistemology of psychoanalysis. After all, Freud unsettled a great deal about our inner world and challenged how we can relate the mismatch of conscious motives with unconscious wishes. In this sense, he wrote against the unitary subject. To unsettle, however, means that a great deal is up for grabs, including any consequent relation between cause and effect, time and timelessness, and the arbitrary and the meaningful. His last lectures, which he could not give owing to cancer of the jaw, continued to insist on the incompleteness of psychoanalysis and its incompatibility with a worldview:

Ladies and Gentlemen,—Allow me in conclusion to sum up what I had to say of the relation of psycho-analysis to the question of a *Weltanschauung*. Psycho-analysis, in my opinion, is incapable of creating a *Weltanschauung* of its own. It does not need one ... it is too incomplete and makes no claim to being self-contained and to the construction of systems. Scientific thought is still very young among human beings; there are too many of the great problems which it has not yet been able to solve. A *Weltanschauung* erected upon science, has, apart from its emphasis on the real world, mainly negative traits, such as submission to the truth and rejection of illusions. Any of our fellow men who is dissatisfied with this state of things, who calls for more than this for his momentary consolation, may look for it where he can find it. We shall not grudge it him, we cannot help him, but nor can we on this account think differently.

(1933, pp. 181–182)

READER'S GUIDE

I have taken on four questions that affect and enlarge our analysis of education: What do the unconscious and sexuality mean for learning and education? What can we learn about our needs for authority and our transference to knowledge from studying the demand to codify and standardize practices in education? Given that schooling occurs in groups, what is group psychology and why should this psychology be narrated? Finally, what might psychoanalysis give us over to think if we think of education's composition as proceeding from "wild education" to unsolved problems?

Our focus is on why an understanding of the play of conflict in psychical life leads to questioning the theories, practices, wishes, character, and dispersal of the concept, archeology, and experience of education. In this sense, our study is an introduction to education as much as it is an introduction to psychoanalysis. A large problem for both education and psychoanalysis is found in preconceptions about their respective work that are so emotionally charged that they come in the form of obstacles to learning along with a refusal to entertain incompatible thoughts. What fuels both debate and repudiation is the fact that both fields inherit childhood theories and begin from homemade concoctions on the hearsay nature of the emotional world of learning and what it means to "teach someone a lesson." Though both fields have as their task a deconstruction of the history of preconceptions and the styles in which they are conveyed, each has a share in conceptualizing a theory of learning adequate to the work of narrating frustrations in learning and disillusioning the afterlife of first impressions. I use the term *wild education* to convey the force and dispersals of childhood theories with attention to their congealment in the currency of contemporary relations and institutional arrangements. The phrasing borrows from "'Wild' psycho-analysis," an early (1910c) article Freud wrote to warn his public and practitioners about their mistaken ideas of psychoanalysis and how it unfolds.

Two orientations structure each chapter: one on style, the other on words. The first develops from my reading of Freud's style of transmitting and revising psychoanalytic ideas. Freud turned objections to psychoanalysis into psychoanalytic objects of knowledge that then returned to the clinic and his theory as obstacles to psychoanalysis. In almost every one of his articles, Freud attends to the difficulties psychoanalysis presents to his reading public, to patients, to his followers, and to himself. So his work begins with the analysis of misunderstanding, accidents, mistakes, and refusals to entertain what is other to conscious life.

It is as if Freud is always addressing a learning subject from the vantage of learning from difficulties. Here is where objections to psychoanalysis transform into psychoanalytic objects such as ego defenses, resistance to resistance, constructions in analysis, moral anxiety and the superego, transference and love, free association, dreams, and group psychology. These "objects," or sticky constructions that describe, recollect, and work through psychological events, are also the outcome of psychology and perform their emotional work. Further, they lend to Freud performative obstacles that pose questions to his theory, to the work of interpretation and, more generally, to his style of psychoanalytic transmission. Objections, objects, and obstacles constitute psychoanalytic movement. From this first theme, Freud's approach is an on-going commentary on the paradoxical qualities of learning and so must accept the rule of over-determination.

The second orientation develops from the influence of uncertainty in words that emerge from a psychology of language, charged with the idea that learning is an emotional situation and tends to be expressed in the subjunctive mood. Freud had as an ongoing focus a psychology of love animated by anxieties over its loss. His view was that love inaugurates mental life, and this raises the problem of the subject's desire in perception, judgment, and imagination. Words and things matter intimately, and they play between the poles of presence and absence and pleasure and un-pleasure. They are felt as in dynamic conflict and as unconscious impressions that create the mind's pathways, associations, and psychical reality. This great flux and mutability permitted Freud to expand the idea of mind into the realm of the psyche, or psychological body. It also gave him free play with the Eros of words. The unconscious and sexuality are the most difficult, contentious concepts in his work and do transform what education and psychoanalysis may mean. They are the most ignored and repressed forces in any education and serve as a magnet for both objections and imagination. Through the force of the transference-love, Eros and the unconscious carry their traces in the charge of learning. In this way, Freud linked education to an unconscious problem of learning for love, to a childhood history of wishes for love, and to fear of its loss. Anxiety, then, may well be a constitutive kernel of learning.

Chapter Two introduces Freud's methods, vocabulary, theory, and preoccupations. His two major theories of the mind are described, with a brief excursion into his metapsychological papers wherein he grapples with the dynamic qualities of the psychical apparatus. Readers may wish to skip the windy section on the metapsychology, although the themes that arise in these thorny pages return in the chapters that follow. Perhaps there is no escape. I try to give readers a sweeping view of his evolving theory of the human subject with emphasis on how this subject revised his theories and affected his style of working. I encourage readers to keep an eye on what happens to education when psychical reality is imagined. A number of well-known objections to psychoanalysis first made to Freud are read as structuring his style of communication and teaching and are treated as objects for psychoanalytic knowledge. Most notable in this chapter is the argument that Freud's style of teaching emerges from his capacity to be affected by the object, and his theory of learning is a testimony to the psyche's halting procedures.

Chapter Three has as its focus the psychology of learning techniques of practice. What Eros is involved in a profession's demand for codifying knowledge of practice? Between 1911 and 1915, Freud wrote a series of papers on psychoanalytic technique, perhaps his most elaborated discussion on the pitfalls and problems of becoming a psychoanalyst. They came on the heels of a demand for a manual and can be considered as Freud's great comment on the objects of psychoanalytic knowledge from the vantage of their difficulties, obstacles, and objections. Freud's novel approach was to analyze the fleeting meanings of uncertainty in practice, not as a problem of application but from the vantage of the practitioner's implication in the technique and the practitioner's style of love. I read these papers as a lively story of education, as a lens to understand our own demands for certainty, and as proposing a new orientation to conceptualizing both practice and theory. These papers are also an occasion to present Freud's theory of the transference, a concept that is at the heart of subjectivity, psychoanalysis, and education and is thought of as animating the capacity for emotional ties, made from the wish for authority, love, continuity, and desire in learning's procedures. In linking a profession's desire for a manual to the problems of the transference, the chapter may also be read as an analysis of our contemporary hysteria with outcomes and evidence-based education, which reduce learning practices to performance objectives and a set of skills to be mastered.

Behavior problems and the teacher's anxiety over losing classroom control are the thorniest objections to learning in school and university life. We want to consider this worried education from the vantage of group psychology and its mythology. Chapter Four turns to Freud's (1921) "Group psychology and the analysis of the ego" and proposes an affected reading of his strange little text. He mentions school life a few times, although the large difficulty concerns the problem of becoming an individual interested in narrating the dynamics of group psychology made from a desire for a leader's authority and love and sutured by member identification. And yet, there are always troubles with following directions. For Freud, following anything turns on the problem of love. Readers will find Freud's changing views on the ego and its defense of identification or the means to constitute the self while proposing its own fault lines. A consideration of group psychology from the inside out may clarify thinking about the education field, where learning occurs in groups and where our commonplace discourses on learning and teaching may well need a depth psychology for a new view on the work, wagers, and difficulties of learning with others.

Chapter Five analyzes Freud's views of education—of children and adults, of patients and analysts, of institutes and schools—and, owing to our wild education made from the unconscious, sexuality, and the drives, brings us to consider education as an unsolved problem. It turns out that learning involves the movements of objections, objects, and obstacles and manages to lend Eros to all these uncertainties. Education—as concept, practice, relation, history, and promise—is caught in the wagers of love, knowledge, and authority, and its mode of transmission is also affected by infantile theories, pleasure and un-pleasure, and conflicts with the pleasure principle and the reality principle. So, we bring to any education the question of why—our threshold to narratives that provoke new conditions for the creation of psychological significance. We will see how Freud's evolving theories of psychical life carry education over to the work of interpreting reality and coming to terms with representing internal and external aggression. We will also ask why conceptualizing education as an unsolved problem permits new learning dispositions. In these ways, we will introduce education.

The educator, once a child, grew up in school and returns there as an adult. From this fact comes the narrative revolt conveyed through the transference: that she or he brings into the present an arsenal of screen memories and forgotten wishes and the vitality of infantile theories of learning for love hastily made from the force of childhood impressions and carried on in anxieties, defenses, and inhibitions (Britzman, 2003b). Here we find one reason defended education feels so timeless, predictable, and aggrieved. Yet, such nagging history has to be made into psychological significance if the desire to take on the teacher's position is to be more than a compulsion to repeat the victories, dashed hopes, idealizations, and disappointments of childhood. Educators inherit the added burden of understanding something that is not education, yet nonetheless leaves in its wake the objections, objects, and obstacles of having to grow up. This wild education indicates both fantasy and a studio for our curiosity. Its other names are sexuality and the unconscious, and they scatter the tattered traces of infantile education that does link learning with the need to be loved and punished.

With his method of free association, Freud teaches his style of inventive readings; it follows that each reader is invited to invent Freud. Free association will be our royal road to introducing education, our means to consider interpretation as linking disparate events into a narrative that at first glance seems like anathema to the procedures of education. Freud invites us to think experimentally with the proposition that education is lost and found within the subject who dreams and fantasizes and who represses and forgets, yet still manages to convey subjected meanings she or he knows nothing about. I hope to show why Freud took all of this "nothing" to surprise meaning.

Like psychoanalysis, the field of education as an unfinished project inherits this other history, or the history of our otherness that must include our trouble with learning from history. Psychoanalytic ideas bring to these estrangements in psychical life an ethic of curiosity and the free association needed to invite narration. Along with Freud, we approach education as archeology and place it under construction.

2

FREUD'S EDUCATION AND OURS

Our right to assume the existence of something mental that is unconscious and to employ that assumption for the purposes of scientific work is disputed in many quarters ... A gain in meaning is perfectly justifiable ground for going beyond the limits of direct experience.

—Sigmund Freud, "The Unconscious"

NARRATIVE RIGHTS

Within the span of two short sentences, Freud posits, anticipates, and defends the existence of the unconscious. "It" irrupts by way of inexplicable mistakes, stray thoughts, and unaccountable wishes and meets with conscious objections. The unconscious taunts intentions and defies justification. It forces the affected ego to reply with repression, one of its many mechanisms of defense. With Freud's presentation of the unconscious, neither experience nor its meaning could be settled. Their estrangement transforms the project of psychoanalysis from that of deciphering the unconscious into creating the conditions for the right for narrative, considered today as an expression of human freedom, as the grounds for imagination and, for many, as the reason why we have education at all.

However, at the dawn of the twentieth century, when the enterprise of science thought of itself as exceeding metaphysics and sought the light of positivism, how strange it must have sounded to announce his newly conceived science with nocturnal affairs under the title of *The Interpretation of Dreams*. Freud's first preface of that book anticipates these objections, and he only adds to them when he tells the reader that most of the dreams under analysis are his own,

> and that I should have to reveal to the public gaze more of the intimacies of my mental life than I liked, or than is normally necessary for any writer who is a man of science and not a poet ... . I can only express a hope that readers of this book will put themselves in my difficult situation and treat me with indulgence, and further, that anyone who finds any sort of reference to himself in my dreams may be willing to grant me the right of freedom of thought—in my dream-life, if nowhere else.
>
> (1900a, pp. xxiii–xxiv)

From anticipated objections comes a reading lesson: granting freedom to thought bestows subjectivity its depth, mysteries, and conflicts.

Freud (1900a, b) supposed the dream to be our most condensed, audacious, and impersonal objection. This nocturnal education returns wild wishes in ways that congeal our senses. He tells us as well that the subject of the dream is the dreamer. The dream also signifies a new psychoanalytic object of knowledge: the unconscious that wishes everything without knowing why. Knowledge of the enigmatic self, Freud maintained, is what poets already represent when they make narrative into a new unconditional freedom: the right to tolerate and represent incompatible thoughts. Science, he believed, must be as bold.

Yet narrative can go anywhere. Beginning with this fact, Freud created a terrific obstacle: he placed into the heart of psychoanalysis a radical indeterminacy by asking, How can the object be read? Our study takes on these literary quandaries by focusing on Freud's inventive style of reading, and questioning what it means to put our psychology into words with attention to the work of representation and interpretation. This approach will bring us to our central question: how does psychoanalysis affect the ways in which we account for our education and analyze the very thought of education?

As for introducing Freud, there is the need to work from within the language of psychoanalysis without securing its meanings. Definitions cannot do justice to the drifts, indirections, and insecurities of mental events. In fact, psychoanalytic language is remarkably fluid. It must be, given the object's lines of flight and the weight living imposes on it. Conflicts between experience and meaning are the psychoanalyst's learning problems. These obstacles to learning become enigmatic methods, resources, and knowledge. Psychoanalysis is instructed by what is most uncertain, by what is unknown, and so by what may be constructed.

All this uncertainty raises the problem of the relation between the mind's mechanisms, which Freud called "the psychical apparatus" and the stories that follow. The original objection to psychoanalysis was how to tell the difference between its descriptions of our emotional world and the theory that presents it. Its language is notoriously sticky. If, for example, we point to anxiety in others, how do we know our own description is not a projection of our own nervous condition? With the idea of projection, can an unaffected observation be possible when focusing on the emotional world? Céline Surprenant's (2008) introduction to Freud's conceptual oeuvre puts the theoretical and practical dilemma this way: "How it might be possible to distinguish between 'things themselves' or 'mental phenomena' and the 'explanations' dealing with their causes … ." (p. 12). How do we tell the difference among the objects of study, our identification with them, and our interpretation of them? To what extent does interpretation repeat variations of an original objection? The trouble is best summed up thus: to think psychoanalytically is to be embroiled in the unconscious.

The dilemma also belongs to having psychology. Psychological capacities are the means to know psychological processes. However, in taking the psychological subject as its own object, the nature of inquiry is doubly affected. Freud thought through this dilemma with his concept of transference; it is as much an unconscious commentary on one's history of learning love as it is a description of the reach of the associative mind. Our return to Freud experiments with these elusive matters and considers what it is like to learn from a psychoanalytic treasure trove of contentions, problems, lacunas, and contradictions.

To work with psychoanalytic fluidity, I follow Richard Wollheim's (1991) insight that Freud's great contribution to both the epistemology and the ontology of the subject was to use concepts found in everyday life and expand, deepen, and elaborate upon their meanings. With the question of meaning's expansion, I add Samuel Weber's (2000) literary discussion on Freud's involvement in his own ideas: "Freud's writing and thinking are progressively caught up in what they set out primarily to describe and elucidate" (p. 1). Though Weber can be interpreted to mean that Freud wrote only autobiography— and, indeed, a great deal of writing about Freud the man applies psychoanalysis to him—from a different perspective, Weber's observation can bring us into the particularities of the psychoanalytic situation: the mind cannot be unengaged from its theories, and subjectivity is a testimony to this strangeness and need for intersubjectivity.

Freud begins with narrative rights. These belong to his clinical method of free association and the "talking cure." He gave interpretations a regard for the "uncanny effects in fiction" (1919c, p. 249), or the imaginative writer's license with fantasy to include what does not coincide with reality as a way to comment upon it. This interest in freedom of language would help explain why he had to take such poetic license, which the mind also takes, and how he would move, by way of his patients' stories, toward the quest for poetic justice. So, "something mental" but not conscious would always be found within theory and practice. Yet, when theory and practice are linked to the unconscious, the motive, evolution, and after-effects of any knowledge belong to a different, over-determined, and so affected order of meaning. Once unhinged from consciousness of it, understanding the indirections of experience, including such events as hatred, love, hostility, aggression, jealousy, and inexplicable thoughts and actions, become problems for interpretation. Not knowing, forgetting, or not wanting to know anything about experience's registrations characterizes the subject's psychical acts, the poesies of mental life, actions in the world, and resistance to psychoanalysis. Indeed, the fragile world of conscious intentions carries the sigh of the ego's mechanisms of defense against anxiety.

Here are two of Freud's most radical assertions: that consciousness is the exception of mental life and that the deferral of meaning is a consequence of the registration of psychical experience, the polymorphous perversity of sexuality, and the ways in which the psychical apparatus develops, thinks, and suffers. We are also facing what is most indeterminate and incomplete about the subject. Things mental and unconscious— lost objects— become the elusive grounds of psychoanalysis, his lifelong work, and in this present study, our impressive means for a critique of education's blind spots made from its reliance on both consciousness and the insistence that we learn from direct experience. After Freud, there will be no education without conflicts and our ignorance. The unconscious will shake confidence in how we come to know history and narrate our own time. With this claim, Freud left us with an irony of knowledge: it will never complete itself, nor will we be cured from what else occurs in our desire to know. Moreover, the conveyance and reception of knowledge will be hard-pressed to escape the knower's poetic license for the transference.

Thinking with Freud means that we need to consider what the unconscious, and so what psychoanalysis, requests from us. This psychoanalytic invitation is strange, uncanny, and cannot do without our objections to it. Paradoxically, objections to Freud and psychoanalysis will provide new modes of psychoanalytic knowledge and the means for this affected knowledge to do its work. As Freud readily admits, but without consolation, the unconscious raises terrific and even terrifying obstacles to understanding what belongs in the flora and fauna of practice and theory. It will muddle our reasons for helping others, bring to the innocence of rescue fantasies their traces of hostility, refuse the secondary logic of consciousness, cause us to lose valuable belongings, and set us going on errands without remembering what we set out to do. From these scrambled events, we will find both the resistance to education and a theory of learning.

Now all of these remarkable epistemological and ontological transformations emerge from inattention signaled by unremarkable disunity such as forgetting names, slips of the tongue and pen, childhood memories, misreading, jokes, witticisms, dreams, and accidents. Between 1900 and 1905, Freud's early work took on these everyday subjects. He began with a self-analysis: the subject who dreams, forgets names, suffers from writing blocks, mistakes friends for enemies, and wishes for recognition. Our everyday psychopathology, by which Freud meant that a meaning is being suffered, is put to work to advance understanding into our most intimate conflicts, fantasies, and condensed wishes. From there, Freud speculates on the problems of happiness and unhappiness.

Additionally, in the early Freud, memory, too—what he (1899) called "screen memories"— no longer corresponds to what has already happened. He will say there are no memories in childhood, only memories of childhood. Memory lags behind these events and even gets lost along the way. It presents as if it were an archeological ruin made from overlays of desire, wish, sexuality, anxiety, fantasies, defense, and the Oedipal myth, all dust of time. He would publish (1909) one essay on the family romance, wherein the child's pressing questions of origin are infused with fantasies of having the wrong family. Memory tells a paradoxical story of forgetting and the difficulties of having to make a past from that strange address of childhood's residency.

In the laboratory of psychoanalysis, memory procedures are unreliable. Forgetting will then include the problem of repression, or the tearing of events with what is most unrecognizable about them. Archeology will be his best metaphor, as screen memories leave behind "no more than a torso" (1899, p. 306).

Freud, too, tried to look backward and forward and considered time as operating with the principle of deferred action, as subject to displacement, and its telling as affected by the compulsion to repeat through actions that cannot be contained in words. He posited something timeless about our mind— the unconscious—a reservoir of impressions, images, sensory perceptions, wishes, drives, and the repressed. The dynamic unconscious holds, fragments, and generates existence. It will be the force of motility for pleasure but will also leave us to our fixations and compulsions to repeat. Because of its paradoxical qualities, the unconscious presented a psychical estrangement to history: it knows no time, tolerates contradictions, and cannot say no. The logic of the unconscious is akin to that of the wish and the dream life. Freud argued that these primary processes create an omnipotent empire, telegraphing our subjective foundations in the codes of dreams, delusions, and mistakes.

Freud's founding problem is with those enigmatic symptoms of the unconscious: the way they communicate strangulated meaning. We are asked to trade-in our imaginary unity and think from our otherness, that strange register of discontinuity, repartition, difference, and suspension. All this leads to the greatest objection we will face: with psychoanalysis, the subject is unconscious. This gain in meaning comes without guarantee. It must be so, as the unconscious ushers in freedom of thought, narrative revolts, and narrative rights. These freedoms that the mind creates expand the meaning of education into new problems of ethics, of having to define, in psychological terms, progress and regression and of considering education beyond the soundings and protests of consciousness. Something other than consciousness drives purpose, reason, intention, and desire. We begin with Freud's claims for the unconscious from the perspective of how he transformed objections to psychoanalysis into psychoanalytic objects and why this transference, as both a psychoanalytic object of knowledge and a new obstacle to thinking, matters for imagining the destiny of education.

METAPSYCHOLOGY AND ITS TRANSFORMATIONS

"The Unconscious" (1915c) is the third of Freud's five theoretical papers known as "The Metapsychology." Written just 15 years into his discovery of psychoanalysis, in it he attempted to sketch the psychology of psychology, or the forces, dynamics, and mechanisms that constitute performative psychical life. The papers expanded his speculations on central motifs: the drives, repression, the unconscious, dream theory, and the work of mourning and melancholia. All seem to lean on the problem of loss: loss of love, loss of reality and time, and loss of self and the other.

From the perspective of the unconscious as a system, Freud sums it thus: "*exception from mutual contradiction, primary processes* (mobility of cathexes), *timelessness, and replacement of external by psychical reality*" (1915c, p. 187; ital orig.). With this logic, Freud will theorize affect, or internal tensions that seek release. His first model for understanding the internal pressures of bodily distress is the baby's cry for the mother. What lends the push into life is his speculation on instincts, or the drives, described in the first paper of the metapsychology, "Instincts and their vicissitudes." There, he considered psychical life from a psychological point of view:

> an "instinct" appears to us as a concept on the frontier between the mental and the somatic, as the psychical representative of the stimuli originating from within the organism and reaching the mind, as a measure of the demand made upon the mind for work in connection with the body.
>
> (1915a, pp. 121–122)

At the time of his development, he posited two instincts: those of the ego, or self-preservation, and the sexual instincts. Both affect the drive to know and are animated by some things that are not biology: love, hate, and ambivalence.

In this metapsychology, new puzzles are made from pleasure, from the excitations of libido, from incompatible ideas, from wish liability, and from the suffering that follows both loss of love and blows to narcissism. It is here that Freud turns a psychology that relies on suggestion and hypnosis into depth psychology and psycho-synthesis and then, in his last years, into ego psychology and the analysis of its defenses and its splitting. This metapsychology, so provisional in its account, takes further direction over the next 24 years from his preoccupation with the affect of anxiety, which he will link to the human condition of dependency, trauma, separation, the loss of love, and transience.

Beginning in the 1920s, Freud reorients the design of the mind, giving to his first topology of the conscious, the pre-conscious, and the unconscious a tripartite structural character made from the associations of object relations, affect, things and words, wishes, and drives. Their representatives take the form of the residual agencies known as the ego, the id, and the superego. His great statement on these matters is found in his 1923a paper, "The Ego and the Id." The ego, the id, and the superego make up an emotional world of conflicted group psychology, culture, and love's impressions. In turning to internal developments, the psychical apparatus then becomes personified and populated by the vagaries of history and resistance to it. Freud found a composite of unconscious education in these agencies and, through the ego's anxiety, theorized the material of character. He gave the psychical apparatus its own force field—conflicts indicating pressures, investments, affects, and object relations, all affected by the drives—and speculated beyond the pleasure principle, or what he initially thought as the rule governing the motives of mental life and the reason for wanting others.

As Freud pondered problems of aggression, anxiety, masochism, and sadism, sustaining his early libido theory—his view, based on dream interpretation, that the wish for satisfaction and the avoidance of un-pleasure oriented the motives of psychical life—proved to be unsatisfying. With his publication of "Beyond the Pleasure Principle," Freud changed his mind on the avoidance of un-pleasure: "This is the most obscure and inaccessible region of the mind, and, since we cannot avoid contact with it, the least rigid hypothesis, it seems to me, will be the best" (1920a, p. 7). He then introduced to his theory the life and death drives and warned his readers what they are in for: "What follows is speculation, often far-fetched speculation which the reader will consider or dismiss according to his individual predilection. It is an attempt to follow out an idea consistently, out of curiosity to see where it will lead" (p. 24). The issue will be the quantities of excitation the psychical system can accommodate and discharge. The life drive was seen as binding ever-greater unities and reaching for complexity, whereas the death drive would destroy, diminish, unbind, and seek extinction. With the drives, Freud presented something unrepresentable about our purposes, reasons, and wishes. He gives the last words to the poet, Rükert: "What we cannot reach flying we must reach limping" (1920a, p. 64).

With his 1926a paper, "Inhibitions, symptoms and anxiety," Freud reframed his metapsychology. His approach is to rehearse his own objections and doubts about his early views on repression. Then came the creation of a new psychoanalytic object of knowledge: anxiety. Whereas he originally stressed anxiety as the consequence and transformation of repressed libido, an aftereffect of repression, the insistence was dropped. Anxiety will be there from the start of life, and repression is not its cause. Indeed, anxiety rewrites the metapsychology with its focus on the ego as organization, as subject to its history of formation and object loss, and as the sum of its defenses, some of which are magical, such as omnipotence, splitting, undoing what has already happened, and disavowal of reality. Anxiety, as emanating from the ego, now takes center stage and will be thought of as a signal danger of loss of love, in contiguity to our original dependency and helplessness. It also signifies a series of losses that accrue over the course of a life. He notes them through developmental stages: loss of the breast, castration anxiety, moral anxiety, and death. Each is linked to fears of annihilation and to "constantly repeated object-losses" (1926a, p. 130). In Part Seven of this paper, Freud writes of his difficulties: "What we clearly want is to find something that will tell us what anxiety really is, some criterion that will enable us to distinguish true statements about it from false ones. But this is not easy to get. Anxiety is not a simple matter" (p. 132).

As Freud's metapsychology develops, subjectivity and intersubjectivity become entangled with forces of Eros and Thanatos, or life and death. The human is susceptible to its wishes and drives, to the dream work, to the unconscious, to love's impressions, to anxiety, to the disappointments of love, and to the external world. This is what Freud meant by psychology and why he proposed it as in conflict with both meaning and experience. In all of this writing, we meet his optimism toward the mind's capacity for the abstractions of thought, morality, and mortality and his pessimism for them when he gave survey to humanly induced destruction, woeful hubris, and the ego's attraction to the unconscious.

FREUD'S PRACTICE

Freud's psychoanalytic career began in Vienna, Austria in 1886, when, after he became a medical doctor and left his research in neurology, he began seeing women patients who suffered from a nervous illness called *hysteria*, and male patients who suffered from obssesional neurosis. At the time, neurotics were most unpopular and were even thought to have a fake or exaggerated illness because, in the medicine of the day, if symptoms of somatic distress were inconsequential to physiology, they had no meaning. Freud had a different view, and the problem of illness as meaning slowly comes into focus in his first publications of case studies (1893–1895) written before the term *psychoanalysis* came into his use.

Between 1893 and 1895, Freud joined with his colleague Josef Breuer and published their cases and theoretical discussions under the title *Studies on Hysteria*. Each man authored separate chapters. Though Breuer created the cathartic method and placed his patients under hypnosis, Freud grew bored with hypnotism; it did not wipe out symptoms, and he tired of constantly saying to the patient, "You are now going to sleep" and hearing the patient say, "No I am not." At first he could not decide whether resistance had to do with the patient, his own poor skills with hypnosis, or the method itself. Significantly, suggesting what the patient should believe did not erase symptoms. It is at this early stage that Freud began to take instruction from his patients' objections, consider the need for rapport and warm regard, and become interested in them. He describes such an exchange in the Frau Emmy von N case. In one session, his questions kept interrupting her speech:

> Her answer, which she gave rather grudgingly, was that she did not know. I requested her to remember by tomorrow. She then said in a definitely grumbling tone that I was not to keep on asking her where this and that came from, but to let her tell me what she had to say ... After I had spoken some calming words about what she had told me, she said she felt easier.
>
> (1893–1895, p. 63)

Freud learned from his patients to listen. He also found a new writing style:

> I have not always been a psychotherapist. Like other neuro-pathologists, I was trained to employ local diagnoses and electro-prognosis, and it still strikes me myself as strange that the case histories I write should read like short stories and that, as one might say, they lack the serious stamp of science. I must console myself with the reflection that the nature of the subject is evidently responsible for this, rather than any preference of my own. The fact is that local diagnosis and electrical reactions lead nowhere in the study of hysteria, whereas a detailed description of mental processes such as we are accustomed to find

in the words of imaginative writers enables me, with the use of a few psychological formulas, to obtain at least some kind of insight into the course of that affection ... namely an intimate connection between the story of the patient's sufferings and the symptoms of his illness ...

(1893–1895, pp. 160–161)

Again, we see variations on poetic license made from the scenery of the patient's narrative revolts.

References to his early patients—the famous cast of Anna O., Frau Emmy Von N., Little Hans, Dora, the Wolf Man, and the Rat Man, for example—gave Freud's theory its startling reach but, over his lifetime, kept pressure on concepts such as repression, infantile neurosis, resistance, defense, transference, and even psychoanalysis. He did not publish discussion on his successful "cases," as he felt learning begins with what is most incomplete, counter-intuitive, and resistant to thought. Between 1910 and 1920, he may have conducted well in excess of 130 analyses of varying lengths (May, 2008).

What did Freud's analytic setting look like? From 1891 until 1938, when an ailing Freud went into exile from Vienna to live out the last year of his life in London, he kept for his clinical practice two rooms of his Berggasse 19 residence in Vienna—a consulting room and his private study. The residence was crowded; there were dogs, relatives, and six children during the first 9 years of his marriage to Martha Bernays. Anna Freud, born in 1886, was the last child. These rooms also contained his personal collection of more than 2,000 ancient artifacts that he began accumulating from the 1890s onward (Gamwell, 1989) and an extensive library in archeology, literature, anthropology, and science that may well have totaled more than 2,400 texts, including the 128 volumes of Goethe's collected work (The Freud Museum, 1998).

At designated times, patients would come to his consulting room; he saw them in the mornings, wrote in the afternoons, and lectured, met with colleagues, or played cards in the evenings. His consulting room had a couch where patients lay down. The couch was a gift from one of his wealthy patients. Freud sat in a chair placed behind the couch, originally because he did not like being looked at. Later, he felt the arrangement gave privacy for both the patient and himself and priority to the drift of words. A patient might come to analysis 6 or 7 days a week, an hour at a time. Some saw Freud only a few times; others, such as "Dora," would dramatically announce that the analysis was over, just as Freud felt it was only beginning. The Wolf Man would never want his analysis to end, and Freud set a date for its conclusion.

Freud's grammar of psychoanalysis would be ruled by paradox and irony, figures of speech such as negation and neologisms, and attention to the work carried on by language: metaphor, metonymy, ellipsis, and slips of the tongue. After all, he requested that his patients say whatever came to mind and become subjects of their speech. His interest in words and things led to quoting with liberty creative writers, artists, and poets and, of course, Sophocles' Greek tragedies. He wrote on the work of Dostoyevsky, Goethe, Michelangelo, and Shakespeare and quoted from George Eliot, Zola, Dante, and Twain, to name just a few. He corresponded with great thinkers of his time such as Einstein, Stefan Zweig, Thomas Mann, H. G. Wells, and H. D. (Hilda Doolittle). His choice of words can even be found in his birthday greetings, such as one sent to Thomas Mann when he (1935) wrote: "I might wish you a very long and happy life as is the custom on such occasions. But I shall not do so. Wishing is cheap and it strikes me as a relapse into the days when people believed in the magical omnipotence of thought" (p. 255).

In 1930, Freud was chosen for the only award he would achieve in his lifetime: the prestigious Goethe Prize. His acceptance speech, read by his daughter Anna Freud, lent to literature and to Goethe their psychoanalytic moorings: "I think that Goethe would not have rejected psychoanalysis in an unfriendly spirit, as so many of our contemporaries have done" (1930b, p. 208). In 1936, on the occasion of Freud's eightieth birthday, the writer Thomas Mann (1957) would address a Vienna audience and celebrate, again, the joining of literary hope with psychoanalysis and, too, give narrative consideration to its other tie, "the bond between that science and the creative impulse: the understanding of disease, or, more precisely, of disease as an instrument of knowledge" (p. 306).

In an early paper on neurosis that argued against theories of heredity and urged psychiatry to leave its reliance on the racist idea of degeneracy and entertain the uncertain world of psychology, Freud first announced, "a new method of psycho-analysis … it is a little intricate, but it is also irreplaceable, so fertile has it shown itself to be in throwing light upon the obscure paths of unconscious ideation" (1896, p. 151). He does not say much about this new method; indeed, its little intricacies will challenge what can even be meant by unconscious ideas. Only later does Freud develop the term *psychoanalysis* more broadly to signify its transcriptions: a movement, methods of investigation, theories of the mind, the functioning concepts and mechanisms of defense against anxiety such as resistance, repression, regression, intellectualization, and sublimation, and the therapeutics made from interpreting the transference, or a radical approach to listening to what else the patient's speech brings to mind.

By 1922, there is an optimistic field called *psychoanalysis*: There were practitioners, patients, objectors, and interested thinkers and centers of education and treatment in Vienna, Berlin, Budapest, and London. There would be psychoanalytic life: congresses, journals, books, child and adult psychoanalysis, analytic training, educational experiments, free clinics, and theories that compete with Freud's views. Psychoanalysis would also affect the creative arts and draw artists into its fold. What is constant is opposition to psychoanalysis. It makes everybody mad.

As for the general public, Freud would write a rather dry encyclopedia entry that set out his movement's agenda:

> Psycho-Analysis is the name (1) of a procedure of investigation of mental processes which are almost inaccessible in any other way, (2) a method (based upon investigation) for the treatment of neurotic disorders and (3) of a collection of psychological information obtained along those lines ...
>
> (1923b, p. 235)

Further, he defined the cornerstones of psychoanalytic theory:

> The assumption that there are unconscious mental processes, the recognition of the theory of resistance and repression, the appreciation of the importance of sexuality and of the Oedipus complex ... . No one who cannot accept them all should count himself a psycho-analyst.
>
> (p. 247)

The entry wound its way into a note on "criticisms and misunderstandings of psychoanalysis" (p. 251), wherein Freud interpreted key objections to his theory as so much misunderstanding stemming from the objector's emotional resistance. In so doing, the consternation made from resistance to psychoanalysis became another psychoanalytic object worthy for inquiry and transformation.

Yet Freud would also insist that psychoanalysis could not explain everything, nor would he assert a final cause that causes every cause because his expansive method takes over-determination as its rule. A great deal remains inexplicable, and Freud's style of defending psychoanalysis consists in outlining its developments, failures, cul-de-sacs, revisions, and ethics. Addressing those who resist is as significant as any other writing strategy he employed for, after all, psychoanalysis is a theory of the mind's unconscious conflicts and cannot do without objections and arguments. His most typical statement on resistance to psychoanalysis comes in a short article, "A difficulty in the path of psycho-analysis:"

> I will say at once that it is not an intellectual difficulty I am thinking of, not anything that makes psycho-analysis hard for the hearer or reader to understand, but an affective one—something that alienates the feelings of those who come into contact with it, so that they become less inclined to believe in it or take an interest in it. As will be observed, the two kinds of difficulty amount to the same thing in the end. Where sympathy is lacking, understanding will not come very easily.
>
> (1917a, p. 137)

He will also tell readers why sympathy is needed: "*the ego is not master in its own house*" (p. 143; ital. orig.). And yet, there is no eviction notice.

By the end of his life, Freud (1940c) returns psychoanalysis to the question of "unconscious ideation," not through dream interpretation but through speculation on the destructive character of waking consciousness. He proposes a new notion of the subject's malady: a split subject, torn in its inner world and a subject who splits the actual world into meaningless pieces. His last problem is with the ego: the "I" who turns away from reality's dictates in such a way that the prohibitions of reality are acknowledged and satisfaction of the instinct is preserved and gratified. It is as if the ego negates its own understanding of its limits by saying to itself, "I know this is the case, but I refuse to believe it." If the ego makes itself from its synthesizing nature, after his theory of the drive, Freud proposed the ego's fault lines: a negative narcissism gravitating toward self-destruction, agonized by the anxiety of loss, and mesmerized by its own perceptions. Through its defensive mechanisms, the ego was thought to have the capability to turn against itself, compulsively repeating its history of losses by shattering or splitting itself into bits and pieces.

What is constant in the early and late Freud's work is his interest in the furthest thing from the mind. In one of his last and unfinished articles, written in exile and dated January 2, 1938, Freud began his discussion of psychoanalysis with uncertainty: "I find myself for a moment in the interesting position of not knowing whether what I have to say should be regarded as something long familiar and obvious or as something entirely new and puzzling. But I am inclined to think the latter" (1940c, p. 275). To imagine the mind in its sleeping and waking states is still to imagine the unimaginable.

As a Jew, Freud was no stranger to the anti-Semitism of his time; it kept him from being awarded a university position for a great many years, and he wrote a number of articles on the problem of anti-Semitism. His tribute to the Jewish writer, Josef Popper-Lynkeus, conveys his personal thought: "A special feeling of sympathy drew me to him, since he too had clearly had painful experiences of the bitterness of the life of a Jew and the hollowness of the ideas of present-day civilization" (1932, p. 224). Freud had never met Lynkeus although he had read all of his books.

In 1933, the National Socialists in Berlin publicly burned Freud's books along with the writings of other Jewish and non-Jewish authors. By 1938, National Socialism would destroy psychoanalysis in Europe, deem it "a degenerative Jewish Science," and ban its practices (Brecht et al., 1993). European Jewish analysts entered a psychoanalytic Diaspora (Steiner, 2000). They moved to Latin America, the United Kingdom, South Africa, the Middle East, and North America. In May of 1938, an ailing 82-year-old Freud, along with his immediate family, paid ransom for their exit visas and left Vienna for exile in London.

A few days before the Freud family left Vienna, a young Jewish photographer, Edmund Engelman (1907–2000), was sent by August Aichhorn to photograph in secret Freud's home and consulting rooms at Berggasse 19, where Freud lived for nearly 50 years. Engelman wrote in his short memoir:

> I remember that I was both excited and afraid as I walked through the empty streets toward Berggasse 19 that wet May morning in 1938. I carried a little valise filled with my cameras, tripod, lenses, and film and it seemed to become heavier and heavier every step. I was convinced that anyone who saw me would instantly know that I was on my way to the offices of Dr. Sigmund Freud—on a mission that would hardly have pleased the Nazis.
>
> The dark day worried me ... . Flash and floodlights were out of the question. I had been told that the apartment was under constant surveillance by the Gestapo.
>
> (1976, p. 131)

Engelman photographed the Freud family, their living quarters, and Freud's consulting room filled with his wonderful collection of ancient artifacts and art. The walls were lined with books and manuscripts and his couch draped with an Oriental rug. As for Freud's building, by the time Engelman arrived, the Nazi flag was already hanging from its rafters. Engelman fled Vienna in 1938 as well, and it was only after the War that he located his photographic negatives. Anna Freud had them in the family's London home.

Once in London, the ailing Freud would finally publish the full text of his controversial study, "Moses and Monotheism: Three Essays." Originally drafted in 1934 and probably revised in 1936, it carried the first title, "Moses, A Historical Novel." The first two essays were published earlier, but he held the last one back. In a second preface to this third essay, Freud wrote of his changed circumstances:

> At an earlier date I was living under the protection of the Catholic Church, and was afraid that the publication of my work would result in the loss of that protection ... . Then, suddenly, came the German invasion ... . In the certainty that I should now be persecuted not only for my line of thought but also for my "race"—accompanied by many of my friends, I left the city which, from my early childhood, had been my home for seventy-eight years.
>
> (1939, p. 57)

The preface ended with a note on the internal difficulties this essay presented:

> No less than before, I feel uncertain in the face of my own work; I lack the consciousness of unity and of belonging together which should exist between an author and his work ... . To my critical sense this book, which takes its start from the man Moses, appears like a dancer balancing on the tip of one toe ... .In any case, let us now take the plunge.
>
> (p. 58)

As a commentary on his time, this third essay considered such ideas as the return of the repressed, historical truth and the mental conditions for freedom of thought. From this poetic license came the poetic justice, for, among other things, his three essays tell a story of Jewish survival.

On September 23, 1939, a little more than a year after he arrived in London, Freud died. The youngest of his six children, Anna Freud (1895–1982), would continue his work. And new schools of psychoanalytic thought began in earnest after World War II. They would diversify and make diffuse Freud's work, taking his inventive reading lessons so seriously that each new school invented its own Freud.

Freud left us to question what is most existential in learning to live and changing one's mind. Why, he asked, does the human suffer from loss in ordinary and extraordinary ways? How does our history of learning return to structure present preoccupations and ordinary modes of perception and thought? What does love have to do with hate? How do wish and desire flourish? What is guilt? Is there really a clear line between the acceptable and the unacceptable or the compatible and the incompatible? What is sexuality? Where does morality come from? These questions of the origin and character of erotic feelings and their particular attachment to ideas and objects could not be settled. Freud said as much in his paper on fantasy and sexuality called "A child is being beaten": "As is well known, all the signs on which we are accustomed to base our distinctions tend to lose their clarity as we come nearer to the source" (1919a, p. 187).

Freud's approach to the monuments of human events was from the shadows they cast in the present. He gave us constructions and tools of deconstruction but, in doing so, placed doubt into his own psychoanalytic project. Essentially, Freud wondered what is proper to our place, how symptoms of epistemophilia carry love, anxiety, and defense, and why representations drive us crazy. However, in taking this particular approach, Freud, too, became entangled in the procedures he tried to represent and, by the end of his career, understood this transference as the only condition for psychoanalysis to take hold of something as elusive, erotic, and fragile as the impressive human mind.

OBJECTIONS

Freud readily used objections to psychoanalysis as a studio of inquiry, as symptomatic meaning, and as instructions that were difficult to follow. The large rule Freud presents is to bring curiosity to the breakdown of meaning and associate to what is most disclaimed, negated, and forgotten. Go on; say what is the furthest thing from your mind. Pay attention, he advises, to what feels like nonsense and cannot be justified. Listen carefully to the broken-off thought, or the incomplete sentence that, on first sounding, defies logic, propriety, and the rule of consciousness. Take courage when thinking with incompatible ideas. Find a meaning in the forgotten word. Study what is on the tip of the tongue. These stray thoughts can be linked to a forgotten history and narrated anew. We are invited to consider the force of experience with the idea that we creatures of impression are affected by what is not known and so learn before we understand.

The most existential objection Freud may have assumed is that a protest against psychoanalysis returns the objector to her or his own shaky ground. Freud came to understand the human as first and foremost an emotional, erotic being, overly susceptible to its immature natality, to its infantile theories of sexuality and to its libidinal capacities for investment. These are the human's vulnerabilities and potential, but they also link the need for love to suffering with its meanings. He added terrors and psychical drives to neoteny, an unconscious registration of our earliest impressions of satisfaction and pleasure. These haunt our credibility, evidence, and reasons. They can leave us in tatters. In the Freudian field, meaning no longer serves as the punctuation mark of experience but rather signifies deferral, displacement, defense, and conflicts.

Certainly, this makes us nervous. However, so does our having to live in the world of others. We are never sure of what we are really saying or how the other receives us; we are subject to runaway thoughts and to experiences we have never had. Also, we are placed in the novel position of the unreliable narrator because things, too, are never what they appear to be. Absence and separation will affect us even more. When Freud transformed the act of receiving the world into a problem of reading into our passionate wishes, he changed our minds about perception, judgment, pleasure, love, and the work of thinking. Perception will become a psychical action in the service of refinding in the world the satisfaction made from our earliest lost objects and the lost causes of our mind. Our thoughts for and theories of the world will never be so far from our wishes for it.

The philosopher Marcia Cavell (1993) gives us a clue as to what may really bother us: "Freud found the source of human neurosis in our long dependency on others and our capacity for symbolization" (p. 1). Another philosopher, David Sachs (1971), puts the problem of introducing Freud this way: "The unconscious, to put it dramatically, first maddens us and then keeps us mad … .Any adequate abstract of Freud's work will also observe that, according to him, everyone is either neurotic or troubled by neurotic tendencies for some appreciable phase or phases of his life" (p. 132). From the side of the psychoanalyst, Julia Kristeva (1995) carries this tradition further: "By identifying with their patients and even adopting their anxiety and excitability in order to identify them more easily, analysts render transference hysterical. We are all hysterics, at least intermittently" (p. 64).

As for neurosis, psychosis, and perversion—all structures of the mind—no one is immune: humanly created ideas and language and our relations to other people, cultural accouchements, natality, the family, and education, for instance, give us our reasons and unreason. These experiences register our affective lives and stretch the limits, designs, and motives of consciousness. Consciousness, or the wish to know things in themselves, it turns out is neither the conclusion of mental life nor even a way to guarantee its own reality. With his structural theory of the mind, Freud (1923a) saw objections as constituting "the body ego" (p. 27) and proposed this agency as more than a bit player on the mind's stage. Whereas the "id" and the "superego" pressure with their own wishes, the ego's handling of internal conflict is carried on through its work of perception, judgment, defense, reality testing, and attaching to the demands of the external world. The ego will stand guard to its own conflictive theories made from a combination of overwhelming internal stimulations and incompatible ideas the world presents. "The ego," Freud (1923b) will insist, "is the actual seat of anxiety" (p. 57) because it is also "the great reservoir of libido" (p. 63) or desire.

We continue to ask why Freud's psychoanalytic theory of the mind makes us nervous. What can it mean for a theory to return us to our insistent and haunting childhood revenants as it asks us to notice the ways we give away our present to maintain what has already past? This is one of the key dilemmas for any education: why is emotional life so incompatible to its projects, demands, and structures? Our entry point is with the question of how psychoanalytic theory, through its insistence on the drive to know and the need to have education, gives birth to learning emergencies.

PEDAGOGY

Psychoanalysis proposes the tenacious problem of education from the vantage of the meanings we make from learning to live. The transmission of his theories to the general public, to psychoanalysts, and to his patients gave Freud over to wonder about the relation between education and neurosis. Yet, he never gave a definitive account of psychoanalysis, left no final word on how it can be or should be conveyed, because the longer he studied the mind, the more mysterious it became and the more incomplete was his theory. His pedagogy proposed education as a question.

Freud (1925a) described and critiqued his learning curve in his autobiographical study. When he first proposed the idea of cure as a matter of the psychoanalyst's transmission of reason and explanation to the patient—what he called, following Breuer, the *cathartic method*—he relied on enlightened knowledge, faith that its transmission can lead to insight and overrule the reign of the neurosis. However, this placed the patient in a passive, infantile position. Even if the patient agreed with the analyst, it was not because of the coolness of rationality and, indeed, this knowledge could return in the form of intellectualization or compliance. Merely pointing out defenses, he found, or telling the patient what was missed inevitably failed. There were two reasons for the failure. Communication itself carries unconscious demands and seems to encourage more objections. Second, the patient is the only one who can really decide the course of analysis. Only when Freud began to listen to objections as instructions for how to be with the patient and as how the patient felt about his or her own symptoms could he disillusion his optimistic approach and move to a psychological one.

The patient, Freud soon learned, wanted the analyst's love. He began to wonder less about the transmission of his own knowledge and more about the analyst–analysand relationship. In his autobiography, which is really a biography of psychoanalysis, he writes: "… the personal emotional relation between doctor and patient was, after all, stronger than the whole cathartic process, and it was precisely that factor which escaped every effort at control" (1925a, p. 27). What turned him into an anti-pedagogue was the way he understood the play of love, hate, and authority as transference.

Freud had a different sense of education when he wrote about psychoanalysis in the university. This essay is one of his simplest and most provocative discussions of divisions in the learning position, and his advice for a curriculum leans on the power of the creative arts to call forth our identifications. He suggests psychoanalysis be taught from the vantage of the humanities rather than from the side of the medical and biological sciences, and "the general psycho-analytic course should be thrown open to the students of other branches of learning as well" (1919b, p.

173). The article concluded with an objection that one would not really learn psychoanalysis from a general course: "But for the purposes we have in view it will be enough if he learns something *about* psychoanalysis and something *from* it" (p. 173). This distinction gradually affects Freud's thinking, as learning about psychoanalysis, as he first imagined its transmission to both his patients and his colleagues, would not transform his own tendency toward needing to settle the conflicts his methods proposed. His early didacticism and rigidity initially led him to require others to follow a curriculum without wondering why there is also a tendency to follow leaders (Makari, 2008). Learning from psychoanalysis, however, would disrupt any smooth transition between knowledge and its acceptance. One learns, Freud came to believe, from identifying with one's own capacity to be curious about what is most incomplete and take courage from gambling with the unknown. One learns by representing an autobiography of learning.

After 1920, Freud's postulation of the conflict between the drives of Eros or unity and Thanatos or destruction, cast the lot of education with tragedy. This pessimistic orientation followed from his second theory of the psyche, now populated by a history of its own education in the form of the agencies of the id, the ego, and the superego. Here Freud situates the human condition as conflicted and as subject to what is inconceivable about the inevitabilities of loss, unhappiness, anxiety, fantasy, and defense. The problem for education is whether its institutions could affect the human proclivity for destruction. Beyond trying to tell students what the world is really like, there were no grand instructions.

For all these reasons, learning is interminable, and this turns the profession of education into an impossible one (Britzman, 2007, 2009). Freud found that both internal and external forces drive reason into the incredulous problem of love and hate and destruction and aggression. His idea of cure would also be dramatically affected: It was no longer dependent upon his correcting ideas or even making proper connections between forgotten causes and present constraints. In the psychoanalytic clinic, learning would become learning from resistances to learning, symptoms most noticeable in inhibitions, anxieties, and defenses that stop short the desire to work and love. When a deconstructive movement now pressures education, it, too, must endlessly slide between the tremors of its own interpretative hopes and the new problems it makes and finds. By joining education to critique, Freud begins to focus more stringently on the work of construction and the capacity to allow psychological significance its time:

> In short, we conduct ourselves on the model of a familiar figure in one of Nestroy's farces—the manservant who has a single answer on his lips to every question or objection: "It will all become clear in the course of future developments".
>
> (1937b, p. 265)

Perhaps the largest question Freud would give to education concerns the problem of time. Without the consolation of knowing its own time and with the insistence that we learn before we understand, psychoanalysis would read the pedagogical clock through its regressions, compulsions, obsessions, and repetitions of childhood. Psychoanalytic timing would also be a strange affair: in the unconscious, nothing would ever go away and so time, for the ego, works through its own deferred action, a retroaction, or the overlaying of the present onto the past to revise both. This retroaction or afterwardness—*Nachträglichkeit*—would be the means to revise and construct the impact of experience felt before understanding. Sexuality would also be subject to its own mistiming: coming too soon in infantile sexuality, disappearing in latency, and returning to adolescence and adulthood.

Even more: passing time would leave behind fossils. There would be for Freud a prehistory, a mythic time that each and every subject would repeat throughout her or his own development. In its nineteenth-century language, phylogeny would recapitulate ontogeny, a history in struggle with the prehistoric and the pre-Oedipal. Each human being would come with her or his own enigmatic archeological site that was called "the unconscious." Putting this into words brought Freud to a new sense of "constructions" made from a survey of ruins where

> Just as the archaeologist builds up the walls of the building from foundations that have remained standing ... so does the analyst proceed when he draws his inferences from the fragments of memories, from the associations and from the behaviour of the subject of the analysis. Both of them have an undisputed right to reconstruct by means of supplementing and combining the surviving remains. Both of them, moreover, are subject to many of the same difficulties and sources of error. One of the most ticklish problems that confronts the archaeologist is notoriously the determination of the relative age of his finds; and if an object makes its appearance in some particular level, it often remains to be decided whether it belongs to that level or whether it was carried down to that level owing to some subsequent disturbance ... it must be borne in mind that the excavator is dealing with destroyed objects of which large and important portions have quite certainly been lost ...
>
> (1937b, p. 259)

His archeological metaphor stands in for shards of experience, wrecked knowledge, tattered memories, and no time. Constructions give a second chance.

WRITING STYLE

More than once, Freud noted that psychoanalysis itself must be subject to interpretation. This rule instructed Freud's strategy of writing and reading and his discussions on the development of psychoanalytic technique. If the technique is to become a mode of learning to tolerate uncertainty rather than be taken as a thing to apply, its meanings would have to be willing to suffer from what the philosopher Paul Ricoeur (1970) formulated as the crises of language, interpretation, and reflection (p. 56). These crises instructed Freud.

Freud's usual writing approach consists of including a rehearsal of objections founded by his colleagues, his enemies, his patients, and himself. At times, he would cast the objector's certainty with comedic flair, as he did in his autobiographical study:

> For years I have been told by "benevolent" critics—and I hear the same thing even to-day—that psychoanalysis is right up to such-and-such a point but that there it begins to exaggerate and to generalize without justification. And I know that, though nothing is more difficult than to decide where such a point lies, these critics had been completely ignorant of the whole subject only a few weeks or days earlier.
>
> (1925a, p. 50)

This problem returns again in his new introductory lectures, published the same year in which his books were burned. In lecture thirty-four, he warns his audience:

> You may perhaps expect an introduction to psycho-analysis to give you instructions, too, on what arguments you should use to correct these obvious errors about analysis, what books you should recommend to give more accurate information, or even what examples you should bring up in the discussion from your reading or experience in order

to alter the company's attitude. I must beg you to do none of this. It would be useless.

But you may raise the question of why these people—both the ones who write books and the conversationalists—behave so badly.

(1933, pp. 136–137)

These objections also work as enigmatic resources for listening that then influence and revise psychoanalytic method, theories, and its therapeutics of depth psychology. Such double action— of theorizing objections and being instructed by them—is the founding paradox in the writing of the history of psychoanalysis, its theory of the mind, and its clinical interventions. However, it also affects any writing about psychoanalysis. If, to return to Samuel Weber's (2000) point, that Freud was caught up in the descriptions he formulated, the same dilemma repeats for those who write on Freud.

One of the most significant claims psychoanalysis gives to education is that resistance and our style of rejecting or repudiating incompatible ideas are not so much the other side of learning as they are the ego's suspicious learning delegates. So, though our interest is to understand objections to Freud and how they instructed him, let us imagine the contemporary objector. Today's readers may feel new scientific fields such as neuroscience, cognitive science, and psycho-pharmaceutics or contemporary theories such as post-structuralism, deconstruction, and feminism have surpassed Freud. These objectors may want only to approach Freud through a strong critique of him. A closer look may reveal how beholden they are to his work.

Freud, after all, asked for curiosity over what we dismiss, including the malingering force of our childhood and the affectations of infantile sexuality. Two points are worth emphasizing. First, across Freud's writing, he related the work of speculating on the nature, functions, and vulnerabilities of the mind to his critics' objections. Second, Freud's writing style contains this double action: in proposing new ways to justify psychoanalysis as a theory of learning, the work itself relied on the mechanisms of defenses this new field of thought brought to attention. Two questions can now be raised: How can any knowledge, including psychoanalysis, be psychoanalyzed? To what ends can knowledge consider its emotional situation?

WHY READ FREUD?

It is worthwhile to ask why writers from such diverse fields such as history, philosophy, literature, women's studies, education, neuroscience, anthropology, the expressive arts, and queer theory, for instance, continue to address Freud's work and his world and why, specifically from the vantage of the topics he engaged, Freud continues to matter. The simplest reply is also one that leads to complications: Freud complicated human interest with its own desire. However, in so doing, Freudian thought polarizes affect with the origin of knowledge and morality, questions our desire for identity through the family romance, reads into our screen memories, proposes a destructive force to life, and provokes profound rethinking on what is most intimate, psychological, and vulnerable within our theories of self and other. By way of his assertion that susceptibility to unconscious life matters, Freud opens subjectivity to what is most idiosyncratic, passionate, and excitable in our being with others and in having one's own mind. His work provides a lens into this unworldly world and then challenges what it is we think we see. We may find that Freud expresses our own fun house mirror, reflecting what we most fear and desire.

Perhaps because of psychoanalytic plasticity and our capacity to doubt it, we borrow his jokes or make him one and still find it funny when our words do the opposite of what we mean them to do. We worry that meaning erupts when we least expected it, that we can forget what we vow to remember, and Freud reminds us that memories can be the site of suffering or their cover. We may hate the idea that there is more in our mind than we know and that our minds wish to be read. Freud introduced the idea that consciousness is the exception, that the ego is not the sum total of the self, and that the unconscious needs neither invitation nor purpose to expose what is inconceivable about our bodies: aggression, drives, fantasies, dreams, desires, wishes, and sexuality. However, for these reasons, Freud is, more often than not, badly taught or hastily covered as a historical figure proved wrong by contemporary science.

Freud's wide-ranging research makes it nearly impossible to separate the man from his work and, now, from our use of him. We tell each other our nightly dream-romps and wonder what else they are about, what meaning they hold in store, and whether these dreams should be considered as oracles, prediction, or after-events that return repressed or forbidden wishes. We find the residues of sexuality in places that are far away from the sexual act. We laugh at Freudian slips, at our bungled actions, at the ways sexuality becomes a double entendre and regularly wonder over the nervous condition of humanity, seeing in others our paranoia, obsessions, regressions, and even psychosis. Further, we wonder about the subject of sexuality: how far its expressions may be stretched, whether education carries its remnants, and why prohibitions accumulate, crumble, and excite. We feel the uncanny and speak of experience through the "*deja vu.*" Freudian imagery creeps into our thoughts, and we have Freud to thank for our awareness that symptoms convey meaning. Even nonsense will cough up some truth. In the Freudian world, poetic license becomes our poetic justice.

Yet, in our own time, the more Freudian thought enters popular discourse, the less understood is his work. This unsettling objection is dismissed by the feeling that we need not return to Freud's writing to see for ourselves what he actually thought, that we can skip over the questions of why psychoanalysis persists in its affairs of love and hate and why psychoanalysis is so entwined with the question of education. That feelings and belief are so close to our earliest wishes for love and our worries over its loss is one of Freud's most poignant and tragic claims. The question of love and its loss of meaning is, after all, one of education's most intimate difficulties.

OUR EDUCATION

We conclude with the question of what education can mean after Freud—how education happens and why we need it at all. Freud narrated education anew when he placed its dynamics within the poesies of the mind: in our conflicts with wishes and desires; in the struggle between the reality and pleasure principles that make up our divided minds; in our libidinal relations with others; in the reach of infancy, upbringing, and fantasies of the family romance; in our proclivities and styles of loving and hating; in the Oedipus complex; in the transference; and in the work of learning the "impossible professions" of education and psychoanalysis (Britzman, 2009). In all of these scenes of love, we can find the currency of anxieties in education and question why the giving and following of directions are idealized, why we take sadistic pleasure in needing to teach a lesson and give failing grades. To freely associate these educational solutions with anxiety in emotional life and the problems of love, hate, and ambivalence may, for some, seem far-fetched. More shocking is to interpret education through the wish for satisfaction stretched to the point of its underside: guilt and the need to be punished.

Freud brought to the very thought of education something utterly new and something alarmingly old. Education, we will see, is more than the deliberations of teachers and students, more than a curriculum to deliver, and more than pedagogy to master and apply. After Freud, education is best thought of through its own psychology and, therefore, as posing new questions. In Freud's view, the mix-up of love and education begins life, and its form will be wild education. His research into representing the bodily mind and his discovery of psychoanalysis as a method of treatment, as theory of conflicted humanity, and as a means for analyzing social life lends a weird abundance to the work of trying to understand humanly created events such as war, art, group psychology, religion, and education. Further, we can use his theories to understand more deeply the neurotica of success and failure and how it comes to be that cruelty, aggression, and violence are expressed in styles of loving and hating and in ethics and morality. From the startles of learning, Freud created a startling theory of learning.

Freud saw reality in our psychical design. He analyzed disbelief but also mendacious belief and feelings of certainty. In what is now known as Freud's last great attempt to trace an outline of psychoanalysis, his opening chapter begins with the limits of knowledge:

> We know two kinds of things about what we call our psyche (or mental life): firstly, its bodily organ and scene of action, the brain (or nervous system) and, on the other hand, our acts of consciousness, which are immediate data and cannot be further explained by any sort of description. Everything that lies between is unknown to us, and the data do not include any direct relation between these two terminal points of our knowledge.
>
> (1940a, p. 144)

What we know is that our knowledge is incomplete because, within psychical life, there is something at stake that is not knowledge at all. It is not only that our motives for knowing and not knowing tell a story of our history of learning and so of our styles of loving and hating. What occurs as well is that the act of trying to know already proposes our self-estrangement. Again, in his last elementary lessons of psychoanalysis, Freud gave a little picture of how his theory is felt: "Its premises make demands upon the audience's attention and belief and very little is adduced in support of them. There is then a danger that a critical hearer may shake his head and say: 'All this sounds most peculiar; where does the fellow get it from?'" (1940b, p. 281).

Imagine, then, a theory that effects the theorist and carries the admission of its own ignorance, its propensity for error and chance, and an insistence that its object cannot really be known without the emotional tie of the transference. Imagine a method that takes its lead from the conflict between theory and practice and invites free association and its narrative revolts. Imagine the audacity to interpret. Then, consider what may happen if what is most inadmissible could be admitted and thought of as composing the human condition of desiring education. If education then becomes something quite other to our plans, objectives, and measures, if education addresses and becomes entangled in both individual and group psychology, it is only because the human self is divided in its perceptions, judgments, and wishes, and this division is a consequence of being affected by others. Such an inward look will take us to startling themes, themselves experienced first as obstacles, then as objections, then as areas of vulnerability for both psychoanalysis and education, and then as constructions for new learning dispositions.

3

THE TRANSFERENCE-LOVE OR HOW NOT TO WRITE A MANUAL

To a well-educated layman (for that is what the ideal civilized person is in regard to psycho-analysis) things that have to do with love are incommensurable with everything else; they are, as it were, written on a special page on which no other writing is tolerated.

—Sigmund Freud, "Observations on Transference-Love"

LOVE

It may have an odd ring to encounter in one of Freud's (1915b) papers on technique a note to love. After all, the way a profession represents its practices—the instructions to carry out, the techniques made for good results, and their promises of logical coherence—are typically split off from the poet's claims, from flights of fantasy, and from both the love it creates and the practitioner's temptations to act on it. Placing incommensurability into the beating heart of practice gives us a clue as to how this love waxes and wanes and why, for the professions, a manual becomes an idealized object.

More often than not, instruction manuals are received like security blankets. They give assurances and protection from the haphazardness of wrong-headed turns. They may even be imagined as magic that can blow away the harshness of helplessness and inexperience, the terrors of mistakes, and the embarrassments of working in a field of insoluble problems. Freud teaches that the wish for manuals is subject to psychoanalysis. Manuals also tell a story of the crisis of education from the vantage of a profession's symptoms, anxieties, and defenses against the loss of mastery. Even techniques of practice become psychoanalytic objects of knowledge and lead to an analysis of love's impressions.

In Chapter Two we approached Freud's education through a study into how his handling of objections to psychoanalysis transformed into the means for the creation of new psychoanalytic objects and object relations. Here, we wonder why the desire for mastery may also be an objection, now against a primary helplessness that is a constitutive feature of subjectivity and the conditions of inter-subjective working relations. We will also clarify how objects of knowledge return as obstacles to psychoanalysis. We continue to focus on Freud's uses of epistemological and ontological obstacles but now from inside his psychoanalytic movement and the problems of the analyst's education. Though learning psychoanalysis poses its own special dilemmas, an inquiry into the analyst's implicit learning conundrums shows that they are not so far away from those of the teacher who must also face her or his subjectivity when trying to understand pedagogical work by encountering others.

Freud's technique papers (1911–1915) were his written reply to the clamor for a manual. The affective experience of learning technique gave challenge: psychoanalytic objects of knowledge, such as the transference, resistance, and even love—all transformations of objections to incompatible ideas—became, in the clinic, obstacles to psychoanalysis. Two questions, under the sign of education, now emerge for Freud. First, how does one become a psychoanalyst as one is learning from psychoanalysis? Here, we need to ask, what kind of learning is at stake? Second, given that the theory of the subject privileges the unconscious, fantasy, and its pleasure principle, how might these forces affect psychoanalytic technique? In other words, what inhibits and urges psychoanalytic learning?

To construct an analysis of a profession's psychology, we will have to imagine that Freud's discourse on love, drawn from his thinking about the ego's design, can be used as resource for understanding a profession's hopes, wishes, and fears. It will mean reading into rationalizations that manuals mean only one thing and that what they settle is uncertainty. Yet, the issue is not whether manuals should exist. Rather, psychoanalysis requests that we interpret our transference to knowledge and look into the dynamics of helplessness. We begin with some of Freud's early views on love, written just a few years before his papers on psychoanalytic technique, and carry them into the demand that he write a manual for psychoanalysis.

NARCISSISM

As much as Freud tries to describe love with impartiality and presents love as an object relation for psychoanalytic knowledge, he also knows that receiving his ideas on love's dispersals and travails is met with incredulity and consternation. That the human passionately attaches to objects, identifying and taking them inside, only to lend libido outward to ideas, people, causes, professions, belief, words, and so on, may be accepted. That the loss of love is where the subject crumbles is also well known, as is the idea that love is its own authority. More unacceptable is his theory of sexuality, his other word for love, and this brings Freud (1905c) to propose, in his "Three essays on the theory of sexuality," that if our nature is to love, there is something unnatural about it.

The word *love* performs its defiance of boundaries. Love can turn into its opposite: hate for the object. To consider these transformative processes as the basis of psychology, however, complicates what is most original about loving. This may be one reason Freud argued that from the perspective of love, there is neither perspective nor toleration for anything that gets in its way. Such ferocity or dedication to love is what Freud (1914b) places into the term *narcissism*; and, its diversions of libido invested onto an object, carry the smitten ego away from judgment and perception, lead to overvaluation of the object, cause it to refuse incompatible ideas, and become engrossed with desires for absolute unity. Love, or Eros, is the great unifier. It is also the human's vulnerability when lost.

Freud's great statement on this matter of loss, "Mourning and Melancholia" concludes his metapsychology. There, loss of love is an inevitable limit for any loving, and the work of mourning carries painful instructions on the terms of object loss. In melancholia, however, the object cannot be given up, is identified with, and is taken into the ego that then berates itself. The ego internalizes the lost relationship with the painful consequence of a double loss: loss of the object and loss of the ego. Here is one of his most quoted sentences:

> Thus the shadow of the object fell upon the ego, and the latter could henceforth be judged by a special agency, as though it were an object, the forsaken object. In this way an object-loss was transformed into an ego-loss and the conflict between the ego and the loved person into a cleavage between the critical activity of the ego and the ego as altered by identification.

(1917c, p. 249)

This "special agency" of criticism would eventually become, in his second structural theory of the mind, the superego. It will still have its melancholic qualities of self-berating and self-criticizing and so serves as a reservoir of guilt and the demand to be punished.

The drive to love, Freud speculated, originates with natality, sexuality, and primary narcissism. Love—being loved, being in love, and loving—inaugurates the ego's expansive domain. There is no way to prepare for love's intensity, nor is there protection from suffering when love is lost. In his paper "On Narcissism," Freud approaches his study through the erotic life of the human and the parents' overvaluation of the child that Freud then named, "His Majesty the Baby" (1914b, p. 91). He goes on to note: "Parental love, which is so moving and at bottom so childish, is nothing but the parents' narcissism born again, which, transformed into object-love, unmistakably reveals its former nature" (p. 91). The paper also mentions other transformations such as ego ideals and idealization: "Idealization is a process that concerns the *object*; by it that object, without any alteration in its nature, is aggrandized and exalted in the subject's mind" (p. 94). Narcissism ensures that the ego is prone to idealization. Later (1926a), when Freud turns to the study of anxiety, idealization will be considered as an ego defense against loss of love.

Though there is strong debate on the advent of narcissism, including its origin, the word *narcissism* is often hurled as an insult or equated with self-aggrandizement and self-preoccupation. The idea that even self-love is a fickle affair is hardly entertained. If narcissism must object to this depiction, we can also wonder what is so objectionable about this mode of love. Freud's construction of narcissism as an object for psychoanalytic knowledge is notoriously complicated, contradictory, and hard to pin down. Today, the question "self image" or "self esteem" inherits these difficulties. The most flexible rule for our approach is the one Freud teaches: handle the concept as a vulnerable structure or as a piece of psychology.

Freud maintained that our earliest love object, the model for love and one's own image, is mother love. This beginning is most impressive, serves with persistency, and gives the first equation of love as the satisfaction of needs. The unconscious carries on this old record, but it also means that, even with the scratches of time, the record can still play full volume. To consider something infantile about the force, attractions, and investments of love's work, however, tends to be felt as a blow to narcissism and as somehow diminishing the individual's maturity, choice of sexual object, autonomy, sublimations, and even the selflessness of altruistic surrender. However, there is yet another way to consider what Freud is doing with the concept of love. It has to do with his key idea that our earliest experiences in love are the most formative and push us into psychology. Their destiny is to extend, transfer, transpose, and transcribe old experiences into new ones. Where psychoanalysis enters the picture is when such extensions turn against the self and become destructive. Love, he wrote in his paper "On Narcissism," is unavoidable: "A strong egoism is a protection against falling ill, but in the last resort we must begin to love in order not to fall ill, and we are bound to fall ill if, in consequence of frustration, we are unable to love" (1914b, p. 85).

Freud viewed the drive of Eros as sexuality, as on the side of the pleasure principle, and as affected by its own influence. His three papers on behaviors in love make these points, and all share the subtitle "A contribution to the psychology of love."

These early papers were written between the years 1910 and 1917 and took on the topics of psychical impotence, debasement in love, and the universal taboo on virginity. The first paper begins with a tip of the hat to creative writers: "Up till now we have left it to the creative writers to depict for us 'the necessary conditions for loving' which govern people's choice of an object, and the way in which they bring the demands of their imagination into harmony with reality" (1910b, p. 165). And yet, the papers are dedicated to questioning why this desire for harmony is so fleeting and why love is always threatened by discord: loss of the object, social taboos, impotency, and hostility toward anything, including ideas, that comes in its way.

PAPERS ON TECHNIQUES

Freud's speculative discussions on the psychology of love from the vantage of compulsions to repeat earlier modes of loving in situations far away from their original context must have been in his mind when he took it upon himself to describe, between 1911 and 1915, psychoanalytic techniques. Whereas technical problems of professional practice are not typically brought into the purview of sexuality or seen as a matter of leaning upon a psychology of love, given the play of subjectivity and reliance upon personal experience that practices in the helping professions involve and eventually turn into worries over boundary violations, deception, and the misuse of power, Freud's approach to discussing psychoanalytic technique involve him with "broken records."

All these papers are posed as recommendations for thinking about the volatility of love. The object love he had in mind was between the analyst and analysand. He named this special love "transference neurosis" and considered it as "an artificial illness" (1914c, p. 154) that psychoanalytic treatment creates and, he thought, must also destroy and work through lest psychoanalysis itself fall into melancholia. This psychoanalytic illness affects both the analyst and the analysand, and love will appear in many guises: as demand, as resistance to treatment, as the analyst's narcissism, and as transference. Additionally, this dilemma that the treatment sets in motion will be our means to understand why Freud links love to problems of education as, after all, his papers on psychoanalytic technique are advice to those practicing the new therapy; and as he meant them as a discourse on the difficulties of transmission, that had to include commentary on resistance to learning. These early discussions on psychoanalytic technique are also contemporaneous with his writings on the psychology of love. Grouped together, they serve as a precursor to his metapsychology.

The technique papers can be read as inaugurating psychoanalysis proper. Originally, Freud planned to write 12. Only six were written: a paper on handling dreams, two papers on transference, a paper on technical rules, one on beginning the treatment, and a paper on the dynamics of resistance and learning. He imagined his audience were physicians, although there were also lay analysts: those practicing psychoanalysis from fields of social work, education, and nursery schools, and those without institutions such as writers, artists, and political organizers (Appignanesi and Forrester, 1992; Young-Bruehl and Dunbar, 2009).

These early papers were neither his first nor his last words on technique, though they still hold true to the central tenants of psychoanalysis. A paper not grouped under technique but serving as a warning device to those about to practice psychoanalysis without learning from psychoanalysis is written in 1910 under the title, "Wild' psycho-analysis." It announced the founding of the International Psycho-Analytic Association and includes his brief statement on the difficulties of learning psychoanalysis: "This technique cannot be learnt from books, and it certainly cannot be discovered independently without great sacrifices of time, labour and success … it is to be learnt from those who are already proficient in it" (1910c, p. 226). In his early (1914a) survey "On the history of the psycho-analytic movement," he insisted on his distinct creation of psychoanalysis and bade farewell to his enemies who were once friends of the movement. Substantial discussions on technique also have separate chapters in his two lecture series: "Introductory Lectures on Psychoanalysis, Parts I, II, and III" (1916–1917; 1917b) and the 1933 "New Introductory Lectures on Psycho-analysis." Thoughts on the problem of technique are also found in his "Note on the Prehistory of the Technique of Analysis" (1920b) and again in his "Some elementary lessons in psychoanalysis" (1940b). However, discussions on method also appear in places least expected such as the speculative 1920a "Beyond the Pleasure Principle" and in his 1925b paper "Negation," wherein he returned to the conflicts between free association and the interpretive license of the unconscious that cannot say no.

Again, in 1937, there were two other comments: "Analysis, Terminable and Interminable," which explored the question of when analysis is over, and "Constructions in Analysis," which focused the dilemma of the work of conjecture with fragments of a patient's forgotten history, now linked to problems of constructing historical truth. His last unfinished paper (1940a), "An Outline of Psychoanalysis," published posthumously, returned again to practical problems in therapy. These last papers were no longer written to a young field, nor did a young Freud write them. However, his approach to discussing technique remained consistent. He continued to link technique to the difficulties of conceptualizing psychical reality in the clinic; he stressed the relational nature of psychoanalytic practice; and he reminded his readers to keep an open mind. Missteps and mistakes were to be seen as places of inquiry.

All his writing on technique admitted key difficulties gathered from his clinic. Behind the scenes, they also reference his disputes with colleagues along with the general public's unease with psychoanalytic propositions on love. His early papers written between 1911 and 1915 are also prescient in another way. Though many of his recommendations seem rooted in his theory of the energetic *libido*, a Latin word meaning "wish" or "desire" and referring to the transformations of the sexual drives, with the technique papers Freud considers the libido's flowering to ask how psychoanalytic theory is affected by and affects the psychoanalyst, the patient, their relationship, and the treatment. Again, he is working with objections to practice and to theory and using resistance as a psychoanalytic object of knowledge and the means to revise its theory and practices. Resistance will come in many forms, he warns. In psychoanalytic treatment, the form it will take is the transference-love.

The technique papers took on the problem of the analyst's psychoanalytic education and essentially argue the case that the analyst will be a slow learner, subject to failure and to the absurdities of practice. They also resided in a question: how can psychoanalysis be transmitted when emotional and intellectual resistance to its methods and theories is to be expected and when the theories as well are constitutive of the conflicts created? Ostensibly, though transmission is considered a problem of conveying his techniques, Freud learned from his work with patients that should he posit techniques as instructions to follow, as authoritative directives to be idealized, or as suggestion, he would already betray his psychoanalysis. Should he attempt to mold his patients into his own image, he would serve only as a parental figure and sustain his narcissism. *Techne*, the Greek term, would be more in line with the conveyance of this dilemma: the arts and crafts of psychoanalysis can be located only in the sensitivities of the analytic relation, and its unfolding dilemmas would provide instructions and critiques of the work.

It is with the technique papers that Freud turns inward and, as discussed in the last chapter, gradually proposes technique as a means to critique the demand for certainty and authority. One great surprise was that just as Freud supposed the love that inaugurates the ego and causes it ill will, this paradox of love became entangled in technique. These are founding problems as learning inevitably involves exchanges of authority, knowledge, and love with the working through of old ideas, with giving up omnipotent defenses, and by confronting the ways in which ideas affect one's conceptual and libidinal world. In a certain way, learning itself may be modeled on the work of mourning, as old knowledge must be given up with courage to attach to what is new and unproven by experience. However, this also means that, at some level, learning is painful, subject to melancholic entanglements, idealization, and self-berating. As in an emotional situation, the learner unconsciously answers to the call of her or his beginnings: learning for love, fear of its loss, and then guilt and the need for punishment. The self-critical stance of learners, particularly in times of both failure and success, is reminiscent of melancholic plaints. If learning can be thought through the problem of constructing psychological significance, we can then speculate on why learning becomes unconsciously equated with earlier scenes: satisfaction and love, and disappointment and the need to be punished. Freud's linking of technique to the problem of love permitted him to consider the attraction to the unconscious in learning.

We shall treat these early technical papers as commentary on the pedagogical problems in the analyst's education, as a critique of the psychoanalytic field's resistance to the unconscious and, more generally, as entrance into the concept of education as emerging from and affected by infancy and its dependency, helplessness, and love's demands. In these last forgotten scenes, education simply means susceptibility to the other's influence enlivened by being cared for, touched, and loved. This is our wild education. These impressions have an afterlife in learning styles, modes of attachment, styles of resistance, and anticipations of the return of the past. They serve as the transit hub in a psychology of love. I want to suggest that Freud's approach to education was made from his attempt to construct its archeology and question its emotional destination. In this sense, how he handles education is similar to his expansion of the meaning, force, diversions, and motility of sexuality.

Psychoanalysis stretches education beyond the conscious plan and elaborates its shadow play with fantasy formation, drives, and the unconscious. Freud observed in the presence of educational relations a compulsion for transference, a repetition of our earliest styles of learning for love. Their urgency is carried by revenants of forgotten childhood fantasies and desires, unconscious demands for love and authority, and Oedipal rivalries. Indeed, learning is best approached as a force field of infantile theories on the origins and anxieties of knowledge and love *and* as confrontation with them.

In what voice does this early history speak? We can answer: with the sotto voce, carrying the force of forgotten situations. Here are some examples Freud gives in his sixth technique paper, "Remembering, repeating, and working through:"

> For instance, the patient does not say that he remembers that he used to be defiant and critical towards his parents' authority; instead, he behaves in that way to the doctor. He does not remember how he came to a helpless and hopeless deadlock in his infantile sexual researches; but he produces a mass of confused dreams and associations, complains that he cannot succeed in anything and asserts that he is fated never to carry through what he undertakes. He does not remember having been intensely ashamed of certain sexual activities and afraid of their being found out; but he makes it clear that he is ashamed of the treatment on which he is now embarked and tries to keep it secret from everybody. And so on.
>
> (1914c, p. 150)

From these complaints, Freud hears the patient's history of disappointed love as transit visa for the analytic situation.

When Freud wrote of the analyst's qualifications, specified the psychoanalytic frame, and warned analysts about the combustible transference, for instance, he had in mind his own missteps in treatment, the internal crisis of the psychoanalytic movement that now held competing views, and the arrogance that composed the young field (Makari, 2008). With respect for the work's complexity, Freud proposed that in beginning the treatment, the analyst think of techniques from the vantage of their play and failure:

> Their justification is that they are simply rules of the game which acquire their importance from the relation to the general plan of the game. I think I am well advised, however, to call these rules 'recommendations' and not to claim any unconditional acceptance for them. The extraordinary diversity of the psychical constellations concerned, the plasticity of all mental processes and the wealth of determining factors oppose any mechanization of technique; and they bring it about that a course of action that is as a rule justified may at times prove ineffective, whilst one that is usually mistaken may once in a while lead to the desired end.
>
> (1913a, p. 123)

Mastery and its illusions will be set aside to go deeper into the idea that any technique will lead to problems of implication and the transference. Mistakes are the royal road to learning and, ethically, any discussion of techniques needs to reference the background problems from which they emerge.

To write freely meant that Freud had to see the transference as a wish for love and so had to return to two of the most objectionable, impressionable, and difficult-to-know qualities of psychical reality: the unconscious and sexuality. Yet, their "techniques" of construction are the procedures of psychical reality. The greatest obstacle to this new theory would be what the theory itself proposed: something mental that is not conscious saturates mental life, knows no time or doubt, follows the logic of the wish and the drives, rejects reality, and divides the subject. The unconscious itself is resistance. This other scene inaugurates the clinical practices of psychoanalysis and creates ongoing technical, philosophical, and existential difficulties, as the subject could not be pinned down and as the analyst's unconscious was a player in the treatment and in the designs of theory.

The same difficulties shadow Freud's theories of sexuality. When Freud (1905c) asserted the primacy of sexuality from the beginning of life, posited the character of sexuality as polymorphously perverse, linked the child's sexual curiosity to the stirrings of research, and gave to sexuality a biphasic time of deferral and return wherein wishes made in childhood fantasy congeal in the adult's desire, inhibitions, and anxieties, he gave to sexuality an expanding unconscious history. He supposed biology through the lens of psychology and, therefore, made a gap between nature and desire. Both the ideas of the unconscious and sexuality, themselves resistance, return as resistance to psychoanalysis. They also changed how learning could be understood, for if childhood is the place of the educational romance, infantile screen memories return anytime one tries to learn, judge the worth of knowledge, and insist one already knows. It becomes increasingly difficult to distinguish between the actual education of the child and the destiny of the childhood of education found in the present (Britzman, 1998, 2003a, 2007).

This convergence of forgotten, repressed infantile education returns in the form of learning for love, most forcefully developed in Freud's discussions of the transference. Within this complex, Freud placed the problem of love. In one fell swoop, he linked the unconscious to sexuality's design and development. In doing so, the new technical problem of the transference evolves: the exchange of love and knowledge made from the problem of becoming one's own authority.

Freud saw in the transference a story about both education and resistance to it and speculated on how stories of life embody both the force of present dilemmas in education and earliest styles of love and hate made while desiring knowledge and needing care. It is this combination of passionately needing to know, wishing for the other's love, and not knowing, that creates our most vulnerable and impressionable childhood. It is also a description of what learning feels like.

GENEALOGY OF THE CONCEPT OF TRANSFERENCE

Freud's conception of the transference is a work under construction. It is a clinical construct that gained from theoretical elaboration of the psychical apparatus, from his focus on the afterlife of unconscious childhood conflicts, from his study of neurosis, and from his discussions on what happens between the analyst and the analysand during psychoanalytic treatment. We find him connecting the transference to forbidden yet displaced wishes in *Studies on Hysteria*. Even earlier his "Project for a scientific psychology," written in 1895 (1950[1895]), speculated on a kernel of the transference dilemma, linked to the psyche's associative pathways elaborated by the displacement of affect from one idea to another. There would be 'thought transference' or the mind's free association.

His technique papers describe the transference as: an obstacle to psychoanalysis; resistance transference; images of infantile sexuality; both negative and positive; ambivalent; combustible material; love; and a means for psychoanalysis to continue. In "The dynamics of the transference," Freud is trying to convince the new practitioners of psychoanalysis about the ego's attraction to the unconscious and its turn toward the pleasure principle. There, he considered that the transference "gives rise to situations which in the real world seem scarcely possible. But it is precisely this that the patient is aiming at when he makes the object of his emotional impulses coincide with the doctor" (1912, p. 104). If, originally, the transference referred to the way the emotional past is registered and deferred through its displacement by repeating a pattern or style of loving and hating in the presence of the analyst, by the end of his career, what is transferred in the transference will be love, given urgency by both psychical reality and the psychoanalytic situation. He writes in "Constructions in analysis," "Our experience has shown that the relation of transference, which becomes established towards the analyst, is particularly calculated to favour the return of these emotional connections. It is out of such raw material—if we may so describe it—that we have to put together what we are in search of" (1937b, p. 258).

Theoretical constructions left over from technical dilemmas and needed errors made in the clinic are constantly transforming transference and how and whether it can be handled. Early in his career, Freud began to notice that his patients mistook him for their family members and slowly began to listen for a certain repetition in ways his patients responded to him and demanded his love, hate, and judgments. Listening meant that Freud had to change his approach to the patient, depending less on clarifying what things meant and paying more attention to what the patient already knew but would not say. This was a lesson taught by "Dora," an 18-year-old woman who was sent by her father to see Dr. Freud and who ended her analysis after 3 months. Freud did not see the end in sight, but Dora did. In a postscript to the Dora case, Freud called transferences,

> ... the creation of a special class of mental structures, for the most part unconscious ... . They are new editions or facsimiles of the impulses and phantasies which are aroused and made conscious during the progress of the analysis ... they replace some earlier person by the physician. To put it another way: a whole series of psychological

experiences are revived, not as belonging to the past, but as applying
to the person of the physician at the present moment.

(1905a, p. 116)

Notable is the fact that Freud discusses the transference from
the vantage of his failure to hear what Dora was saying to him:
"I did not succeed in mastering the transference in good time"
(p. 118). In thinking about his own failure, he writes that the
transference will be the most difficult for the analyst to interpret
because what is conveyed are styles of loving and hating found
in dreams; in choice of words; in infantile theories of sexuality,
authority, and knowledge; and even in stories told that seem to
have nothing to do with the analyst. The transference comes
only in the form of clues carried by feelings of immediacy that
effectuate, for both the analyst and the analysand, a strong
sense of urgency to act rather than to analyze. It is as if, in the
transference, we are always speaking to the wrong person or
replaying old disappointments without relating them through
the currency of contemporary psychological significance.
Oddly, the transference will be the work of disclaiming both
the past and the present. Eventually, Freud will consider the
transference as the greatest obstacle to psychoanalysis and
its most imaginative object of knowledge dedicated to the
construction and disillusionment of wild education.

After Dora, the transference becomes the heart of the
analytic situation, and interpreting it will lean as much upon the
analyst's own analysis as it does on learning tact. This is because
the analyst's conviction about the pervasive and persuasive
transference is first learned not from study of the idea but
from the feelings made while being a patient in analysis. In
both Freud's time and now ours, two further difficulties with
defining the transference occur. First, as a central concept, it
has become so affected by a history of debates that one must
wonder: are there communications that are not beholden to the

transference? Second, because the transference plays out in the analytic setting, one is bound to ask: what, then, is the difference between transference and love?

What can be noticed is that the transference, or the ways each individual lends interest and suppositions to others, is oriented by the timelessness of the unconscious, its refusal of contradictions, and its tendency toward symbolic collapse. Its jumble of impressions of loving and hating renders perception libidinal. These impassioned processes compose the psychoanalytic situation as well and so pose technical problems and theoretical concerns. In the judiciously titled "The dynamics of transference," Freud attempted to sketch its qualities, force, resistance, and unconscious logic as it played in the clinical setting. There, he wrote that though outside the treatment transference is pervasive, "The erotic transference does not have such an inhibiting effect in institutions, since in them, just as in ordinary life, it is glossed over instead of being uncovered" (1912, p. 106). This early paper ends with the idea that the transference is a turn away from reality and is best summed up through wish perception or what Freud called, "forgotten erotic impulses immediate and manifest" (p. 108).

Three years later, Freud proposed more difficulties, with a focus not on the psyche's structure and mechanisms but on the analyst's desire. "Observations on transference-love" takes on the problem of falling in love in analytic treatment. It can go either way: the analyst can fall in love with the patient or the patient with the analyst. Freud then argues that this transference is the most difficult clinical challenge, as it aims at the analyst's narcissism, itself an obstacle to learning. There are many ways the analyst can fail:

> It has come to my knowledge that some doctors who practise analysis frequently prepare their patients for the emergence of the erotic transference or even urge them to "go ahead and fall in love with the

doctor so that the treatment may progress." I can hardly imagine a
more senseless proceeding.

(1915b, p. 161)

There is no preparation for falling in love, and it comes with
its own urgent manual of convictions.

With all of these problems, Freud recommends the analyst
treat the transference as real in the sense of its psychical
reality and as a consequence of the psychoanalytic situation
rather than as a realistic portrait of the analyst as a person.
He advises analysts to allow the erotic transference to persist
without promises of action, false morality, or any illusion that
distorts the psychoanalytic ethic of truth. If what qualifies the
transference-love is the analytic situation and resistance to it,
this is because love involves the self in the disregard of reality,
magical thinking, the overvaluing of the object, a refusal to
consider another way of thinking, and an urgency to act. All
this erotic confusion is caught in everyday phrases: "falling head
over heels," "being smitten," "walking on clouds," and "falling
madly in love." The work is to analyze these events.

THE DEMANDS

The transference is a real piece of emotional, erotic life; it comes
in many forms, including the demand for a manual. On the
heels of these technique papers, the psychoanalytic movement
was embroiled in a series of disputes, theoretical disagreements,
and divergent practices. Freud (1914a) rehearses this crisis
in his revisionist history of the movement. Some in Freud's
circle wanted a manual to stabilize psychoanalytic processes,
secure the qualifications of the psychoanalytic movement, and
distinguish psychoanalysis from other therapeutic practices.
Others wanted to know what Freud actually did in his clinic.
Still others wanted to learn the method. The wish was for a

manual to unify the psychoanalytic movement, and this wish for unity and a practice without conflicts looks suspiciously like the work of love. It is also a profession's best defense against its own anxieties.

The pressure to secure and standardize the new method of psychoanalysis was also affected by daily crisis: there were profound breakdowns over schools of thought, breaches of loyalty, boundary violations, accusations of quackery and, in the psychoanalytic field, hysterical theory wars that traded in projections, paranoia, and insults. To be sure, the history of psychoanalysis is littered with lost friendships over disputes in the meanings and relevance of psychoanalytic concepts; refusals to accept the nature, force, and status of sexuality and the unconscious; and dissent over the causes, reasons, and logic of suffering and cure. These Oedipal rivalries are also the inevitable conflicts that compose group psychology; yet, the affective force of these conflicts, acted out before they can be remembered, reverberate within the play of the passionate transference. Freud's vast archive of letters documents these scenes and disappointments along with misalliances, malfeasance, and therapeutic failures.

Another scene was the anti-Semitism of Freud's time. He seemed to always worry that psychoanalysis would be labeled as a Jewish science and, in the language of anti-Semitism, would be considered as an indicator of degeneracy, a persistent charge that reached its terrible apex in National Socialism (Goggin and Goggin, 2001). In a short paper on "Resistances to psychoanalysis," Freud admitted that along with the emotional resistances were intellectual ones and that "powerful human feelings are hurt by the subject-matter of the theory" (1925e, p. 221). There were also social prejudices and external difficulties. His essay concludes with personal thoughts on society's negative transference to psychoanalysis and to himself:

Finally, with all reserve, the question may be raised whether the personality of the present writer as a Jew who has never sought to disguise the fact that he is a Jew may not have had a share in provoking the antipathy of his environment to psycho-analysis ... . Nor is it perhaps entirely a matter of chance that the first advocate of psycho-analysis was a Jew. To profess belief in this new theory called for a certain degree of readiness to accept a situation of solitary opposition—a situation with which no one is more familiar than a Jew.

(1925e, p. 222)

No manual could ever prepare practitioners for such hostility, negative transference, and aggression, nor could it ever anticipate the unreality social hatred puts into place.

WITH TECHNICAL PROBLEMS COME EXISTENTIAL ONES

Like Freud, we will treat this object of education—namely the manual— in the following way: as emerging from objections, as a piece of group psychology with its need for a leader, as signifying a profession's unconscious wish for absolute knowledge, and as a defense against crisis. Demands for a manual seem to be one solution to a profession's anxiety, although they hark back to the wish for the parent's authority, to the child's fantasy of the parent as capable of mind-reading powers, and our capacity to regress in the face of uncertainty. This story of the transference will repeat these infantile conflicts, as wishes take liberty with chronology. Finally, the paradox of the transference—that there can be no learning without the transference but that the transference is an obstacle to learning—gives us a clue as to why knowledge is idealized or so subject to disparagement when it disappoints.

One problem a manual was thought to settle is how one could become an analyst in a field always being constructed and even dissembled by the workings of its objects and by the nature of relationships it constructs. How its theories could be transmitted and learned, however, paled in the face of urgent learning demands. The closest Freud (1919b) came to thinking about a psychoanalytic curriculum carries the title "On the teaching of psychoanalysis in universities." In Chapter Two, I noted his essay's closing remarks. Now, let us look into the stakes in the conflict between learning about psychoanalysis and learning from psychoanalysis. Both directions animate love and hate and are conveyed through the transference: affects linked to unconscious fantasies or thought perceptions made from having to grow up in families and schools, where we love before we learn and learn before we understand. The erotic transference carries on our earliest preconceptions of infantile learning. To reach into this psychological underworld, Freud's essay on teaching psychoanalysis in the university advised those interested in the work of trying to understand the congealed motives of emotional life to engage with art, myths, and literature. There, affects are given their inextricable free play and cathartic force. To understand something of their fate, we must read between the lines.

Freud's (1919b) essay on psychoanalysis and the university may now be read as a flight of fantasy, as psychoanalysis did not live there and, owing to anti-Semitism, his 1885 application to teach there languished in the dead-letter office. Only in 1902, after a colleague's wife intervened with a bribe to an official, did he become "Professor Freud" (Breger, 2000, p. 163). Another fantasy on the question of teaching psychoanalysis may have to do with how Freud imagined the education of analysts from the vantage of the future of psychoanalysis. His imagined curriculum would place science into question with the insistences of the arts and today can be seen as one force of interdisciplinarity, a contemporary conflict in the university. As for questions of teaching, it turns on the problem of learning. How, without knowing the destiny of learning the work, does one prepare for its experiences of uncertainty, revision, and resistance? It is almost like trying to prepare to fall in love.

Another reason Freud wished psychoanalysis would have a place at the university was that though the practice of psychoanalysis was the movement's "bread and butter," he believed that its significant contribution would go beyond the intimacies of the clinic. Psychoanalysis was created not only to affect individual neurosis but to understand these emotional conflicts in social policy, in institutional life, in cultural practices, and in studies of religion, social violence, and war. Yet, even with these grand plans, Freud set himself another limit to its education. He felt psychoanalysis could never be a *Weltanschauung*, or total worldview. In a discussion on the status of psychoanalytic knowledge, Bass (1998) presents Freud's paradox: "As the science of the unconscious processes, psychoanalysis will have to explain why the wish for a *Weltanschauung* is perennial, and why the gratification of such a wish is inimical to psychoanalysis" (p. 417). In this sense, a manual could become an assertion of a worldview. From the educational side, manuals can be unconsciously linked to the infantile wish for an absolute knowledge, so indexing a piece of psychoanalytic transference. Any desire for certainty could mean only that something was terribly uncertain.

Freud knew that a manual could serve only as a defense against psychoanalysis. Here is where education begins to transform from a worldview into a set of conflicts. Three conflicts of the transference that pertain to learning are worth noting. The first has to do with the problem of setting up a school of thought and practice dedicated to uncertainty and to the capacity to be affected by the unconscious. A second tension flowers in the fact of the elusiveness of the psychoanalytic objects themselves—dreams, transference, and fantasy—all emotional situations indexing wish, anxiety, and defense. These object relations are subject to displacement, misrecognition, and timelessness. A third tension belongs to the transmission of practice, or the formation of the analyst. The analyst constructs meaning by interpreting the force of his or her own unconscious and its drives. Now each of these conflicts risks the return of the repressed: infantile fantasies of education and their tendency to both overreach and destroy meaning. So, education itself would have to be imagined as destabilization and as a deconstruction of its red-hot underside: the desire to help, to rescue, to mold, to idealize, and to cure. These three conflicts of transference—school formation, the return of the repressed, and the analyst's education— mean that psychoanalysis would have the interminable task of questioning and analyzing its own unfolding, handling the volatility of the transference with the uncertainty of constructions.

As for the rush to practice this new science, which must have felt like living in an unfinished house without noticing the danger signs, this too was transference. Instead of a manual, Freud's compromise was in the form of technical recommendations on the problems of learning from psychoanalysis. So he warned psychoanalysts against thinking they knew what was best for their patients and recommend they settle instead for something modest and less certain: learning with the patient by letting the material emerge without telling her or him how to think of it. Here are Freud's thoughts on the psychoanalytic cliché:

> ... but what a measure of self-complacency and thoughtlessness must be possessed by anyone who can, on the shortest acquaintance, inform a stranger who is entirely ignorant of all the tenets of analysis that he is attached to his mother by incestuous ties, that he harbours wishes for the death of his wife whom he appears to love, that he conceals an intention of betraying his supervisor, and so on! ... I must warn everyone against following such examples.
>
> (1913a, p. 140)

What then could be said about the practice of psychoanalysis? The conundrum was terrific: if the analyst believes she or he can help someone out of their conflicts with promises of betterment and progress, the analyst will only repeat the problem. Here we have one quality of the transference neurosis. The method is affected by this constitutive failure, which eventually, 10 years after the papers on technique, brought Freud (1925d) to link resistances to psychoanalysis to its status as one of the impossible professions. Surely all of this led discussion on the nature of the work from the vantage of its difficulties: inevitable problems, dilemmas, dangers, and paradoxes of learning that the method itself created and revised.

The power of the transference also caused Freud to rethink the handling of dreams. He came to worry that his distinction between the dream's manifest and latent content would become a psychoanalytic mantra used to settle its meaning, thereby destroying the analyst's stance of not knowing, or what he called "neutrality." In a footnote to *The Interpretation of Dreams*, added in 1925, Freud cautioned analysts on their desire to interpret the dream's latent meaning and even advised them to question their motives in holding to the idea that dreams can be interpreted and put to rest with the analyst's knowledge of their meaning. This, too, was a piece of transference, a means to settle the unknown and oddly forget one's history of trying to know. He insisted on something more elusive: "At bottom, dreams are nothing other than a particular *form* of thinking, made possible by the conditions of the state of sleep. It is the *dream-work* which create that form, and it alone is the essence of dreaming—the explanation of its peculiar nature" (1900b, p. 507). Even Freud's claim that dreams were wish fulfillments caused a great deal of misunderstanding, for the wish in the unconscious, or what we would see today as desire, is itself a product of the dream-work dedicated only to distorting and displacing forgotten pieces of history.

If at first Freud agreed to write a manual, the more he tried to describe psychoanalysis, the more he understood that a manual would only sustain the illusion of knowing, dedicated to infantile theories of education. His approach was to assure the analyst that he or she will fail if the analyst desires to correct, feels she or he knows better, relies on the force of his or her own personality and authority, and forgets the dream-work. This, after all, was what Dora taught Freud. However, no matter how neutrally Freud's technique papers attempted to describe the reasoning and frame of the therapeutic techniques of psychoanalysis or how the analysis was to be conducted, all of his advice turned on what will be the most difficult feature: the relationship between the analysand and the psychoanalyst. Everything depends upon and falters within the transference-love between them.

In placing the problem of love into the clinic, by seeing love as the force of both cure and suffering, and through identifying its combustible, volatile qualities, Freud seemed to be asking the analyst to play with fire rather than learn how to light a match. It is here that the analyst's and teacher's roles become comparable. Like the analyst, the teacher is there waiting for students and meets with them on a daily basis. The teacher is also subject to the student's fantasies and does learn to tolerate half-baked thoughts and find something other than meaninglessness by wondering what else the student may be conveying when the student gives compliments, leaves a nasty note, or forgets to hand in homework. If the classroom, like the clinic, seems to call on the teacher's authority, how authority is handled trades on the teacher's interest in the student's willingness to think and become a participant in learning. Finally, the transference carnival is also an index of love and hate between the student and the teacher. The analytic problem both education and psychoanalysis share is how to understand the style of love the transmission of practice leans upon.

Just how real is the transference? Can this relationship in its entirety stay put in language and be contained by interpretation? If the transference is unconscious yet justifies its truth through urgent feelings of love, how would the analyst determine the differences between fantasy and reality in the clinical session? What fantasy is at stake here? What is it to act out the transference, and why might the analyst be subject to the transference in ways that are barely discernable yet nonetheless convincing?

These questions, too, are not so far away from our contemporary field of education and its concerns with the teacher's sexuality, the student's sex education, boundary violations between teachers and students, worries over touching students, suspicions toward male teachers in nursery and elementary schools, and fears over the acting out of moral turpitude. Yet, the relation between education and Eros, whether it be conveyed by the student's demand for the teacher's love or the teacher's demand to be loved by students, also indicates that the transference is alive and well in pedagogical scenes. The teacher is interested in the students and calls their transference. The tension is that no manual can settle the problem of intersubjectivity, no manual can tell one how to predict the thoughts and reasoning of the teacher and student, and no manual can direct what education feels like or tell us why emotions rule and break the heart of learning.

FROM TECHNIQUE TO TECHNE

Freud's (1914c) "Remembering, repeating and working-through" is perhaps his most pedagogical attempt to depict the problem of learning in psychoanalytic treatment. The paper begins with reminding new and old readers of the changes in psychoanalysis. Techniques, after all, do not fall from the sky but themselves reference a history of development, failure, and controversy. He described what at the time was the short history of technique for, after all, when this paper was published, psychoanalysis was barely 14 years old and still trying to emerge from its optimistic phase.

At first, Freud tied remembering to an early goal of psychoanalysis, the cathartic method whereby, through hypnosis and suggestion, the patient remembered a forgotten trauma, which originally was thought of as the repressed memory and the root of the symptomatic illness. Remembering, however, was not curative because of its tendency to search for a single event and secure a cause. It was of no use to understanding the complexity of symptoms as a story of current life. Hypnosis and suggestion were abandoned.

Freud's second approach developed from a focus on having the patient repeat what was not remembered through the fundamental rule known as *free association*. Without the security of judgment or censorship, the patient was urged to say anything that came into the mind. However, free speech, too, gave way to resistances, or objections, to the mind's content. Freud then noticed that these surface objections, indicators of repression, were repeated in particular ways. The repetition involved not ideas but affect signifying styles of loving and hating in early relationships. This history of dependency was being transferred onto the presence of the analyst. Interpretations of resistance, then, were made. Yet just as the earlier cathartic method could not wipe away symptoms, Freud wrote that

> ... giving the resistance a name could not result in its immediate cessation. One must allow the patient time to become more conversant with this resistance with which he has now become acquainted, to *work through* it, to overcome it, by continuing, in defiance of it, the analytic work according to the fundamental rule of analysis.

(1914c, p. 155)

Working through, then, would become Freud's understanding of technique itself and his third model for psychoanalysis. He would rely on objections to instruct him and, in this approach, would not only stretch the discipline and designs of science into the world of fiction, belief, illusion, and disillusion. Working through would also become a means for understanding the work of mourning losses, sublimation, and creativity. It would provoke a new theory of transference, from the vantage of conveying a style of learning always under construction, yet threatening to collapse from the weight of love.

These technical papers tell a story of runaway knowledge, itself a quality of the transference. There is a great distance between the analyst's knowledge of the mind and the patient's knowledge of life. Interpreting conflict does not necessarily serve as a bridge between them, so the analyst may as well accept difference and uncertainty as the conditions of the work. Theoretical knowledge, then, comes to serve as the analyst's restraint and proposes an ethic of thinking as a pause on the urgency to act. Psychoanalytic theory would become only the ideas one thinks with, used as corrections or, at the very least, for the analyst to understand her or his hand in the inevitable mistakes made in the talking cure. The patient's speech scenery is where the participation, transference, constructions, and understanding will emerge. Respecting this difference and, indeed, conflict between theory and practice will allow the patient a chance to ally with the analyst and usher in a new learning position that Freud (1914c) also called an "artificial illness" (p. 154) or the transference neurosis. This peculiar playground of transference, though built from the analysand's inchoate demand for love, will also be where this new illness can be analyzed.

Learning psychoanalysis, Freud teaches in his technique papers, could proceed only by way of breakdown and retroaction. Within the folds of practices and theories are the conflicts, anxieties, fantasies, and defenses that compose the mind and self/other relations. Psychoanalysis narrates their unfolding but is affected by this. The largest complication of the difficulties psychoanalysis presents belongs to the 23 volumes— *The Standard Edition of the Complete Psychological Works of Sigmund Freud*—and the writing can be read as performing what is interminable about a manual with a discourse on the conflicts we have with following instruction.

FREUD'S EDUCATION ENCORE

When a 60-year-old Freud was asked how he came to choose his life work and so began by reflecting on his own schoolboy psychology, he presented a story of his transference to the authority of school and teachers, forever linking the transference to the very thought of education (Britzman, 2009). His archeological excursion led him to notice his love affair with knowledge yet to be learned, and he found his incredulity at having to learn again that school memories still affected his present feelings. His opening remarks to this essay can be read as what the transference to education feels like:

> It gives you a queer feeling if, late in life, you are ordered once again to write a school essay. But you obey automatically like the old soldier who, at the word "Attention," cannot help dropping whatever he may have in his hands and who finds his little fingers pressed along the seams of his trousers. It is strange how readily you obey the orders, as though nothing particular had happened in the last half-century. But you have grown old in the interval.
>
> (1914d, p. 241)

If the transpositions of authority are one part of the story of the transference, the other part—love—breaks open its timing. Incommensurable love writes on a different page. In turning to his schoolboy psychology, Freud admitted that he did not know which affected him more: what the teacher taught or what the teacher was like. When it came to his memories of schoolboy education, he was fairly sure that teachers ignored the students' emotional use of them, although on reading Freud's passionate description, it seems odd to be so blind to this family romance. His next memories are made from events that play behind the backs of his teachers but nonetheless involve them: flights of fantasy life that write a manual with invisible ink:

> We courted them or turned our backs on them, we imagined sympathies and antipathies in them which probably had no existence, we studied their characters and on theirs we formed or misformed our own. They called up our fiercest opposition and forced us to complete submission: we peered into their little weaknesses, and took pride in their excellences, their knowledge and their justice. At bottom we felt a great affection for them if they gave us any ground for it, though I cannot tell how many of them were aware of this.
>
> (1914d, p. 242)

What else occurs behind the scenes of education, we surmise, only sets the stage for love's learning. However, the scenery should also be studied. The students did not have to be taught how to rehearse their parts, and no manual could prepare the teacher for what else happens in this group psychology because of the passion plays of the transference.

Readers are advised to keep Freud's schoolboy description in mind for Chapter Four, a minefield of group psychology.

4

GROUP PSYCHOLOGY AND THE PROBLEM OF LOVE

It is true that individual psychology is concerned with the individual man and explores the paths by which he seeks to find satisfaction for his instinctual impulses; but only rarely and under certain exceptional conditions is individual psychology in a position to disregard the relations of this individual to others. In the individual's mental life someone else is invariably involved, as a model, as an object, as a helper, as an opponent; and so from the very first individual psychology, in this extended but entirely justifiable sense of the words, is at the same time social psychology as well.

—Sigmund Freud, *Group Psychology and the Analysis of the Ego*

EXPECTING PSYCHOLOGY

We see in the foregoing epigraph Freud's style of extending individual psychology into an analysis of the social order. Words are his best justification, but they also carry ambiguity. Assuming an intimate relation between group and individual psychology, does the individual give its psychology to the group or is it the other way around? Freud's 1921 study, *Group psychology and the Analysis of the Ego*, transforms this question and plunges readers into the thickets of psychological entwinement and the struggle for separation. Freud's text is difficult, perhaps even a form of disregarding real relations to his readers. This present chapter, too, may carry such dilemmas. Readers are invited to experiment with the preceding remarks and ask: what are the exceptional conditions whereby individual psychology may disregard its real relations to others? What forms can this disregard take? We develop these questions throughout this chapter but for now can notice the complications Freud already proposes: the unconscious disregards real relations to others, the transference holds this disregard in store, and some of the ego's defense mechanisms such as denial and undoing what has already happened can be grouped here as well. In the last chapter, we also proposed that free association in the psychoanalytic clinic invites disregard for the real feelings of the analyst and others. Freud creates more forms of disregard in his little book. We pick up this last thread in the chapter's conclusion.

By design, Freud's term *group psychology* is slippery, and this has not gone unnoticed. It can index the modalities, swings, and influential power of social mood, common feelings, and cultural interdictions. As an indication of conflict, it sways between regard and disregard with the world on offer. The idea of psychology characterizes group dynamics and anticipations but is also a way into a narrative that works through the ways a group sutures rules and justifies procedures for exclusions and explosions. Psychology is as much a story of passionate attachment within the group as it is a struggle for separateness. So group psychology may also signify the divisions of the ego's internal world and the conflicts its defenses propose. From any of these angles, group psychology invokes problems of love, hate, and ambivalence.

Freud's first foray into psychoanalysis of cultural life— "Totem and Taboo"— was an attempt to account for the psychological features of laws, institutions, sacred objects, and prohibitions. He wrote of the study's experiment with analysis of cultural life as "a first attempt on my part at applying the point of view and findings of psycho-analysis to some unsolved problems of social psychology [*Völkerpsychologie*]" (1913c, p. xiii). It is difficult to imagine which unsolved problems he had in mind. His 1921 study, however, took a different approach with representing unsolved problems, now from the vantage of what can be learned from ego psychology in relation to the group.

As with his first attempt to bring psychoanalysis into cultural relevance, Freud's strange little book, *Group Psychology and the Analysis of the Ego*, presents to contemporary readers a number of reading conundrums punctuated by the question as to whether to dismiss it with a litany of objections. Should this book be considered as outmoded, archaic, and fantastical? Or, can these terms themselves—the archaic, the fantastic, and the outmoded—be considered as the echoes of psychical reality? Within contemporary psychoanalysis there is puzzlement as to how to read this text and uncertainty as to where to place it within Freud's clinical and theoretical writing (Person, 2001). In chronology, it comes in the middle of his evolving theory and may be read as a transition between libido theory and his move into unsolved problems of anxiety. The text itself is uncanny. These feelings of frustration may pertain to the reach of his theory, now into the subterranean depths of social psychology to clarify the dilemma of ego formation. Readers may wonder whether Freud is taking ideas too far: his attempt to represent primary logic of group life manages to both alienate and suspend meaning.

We have seen these objections before; the previous chapters proposed Freud's method as the transformation of objections to psychoanalysis into psychoanalytic objects of knowledge and then considerations of how these constructions carry into the clinic obstacles to psychoanalysis. These are Freud's primary means of extending his ideas, and they characterize his way of breathing life into them. With this 1921 study, clinical constructs such as identification, the drives, and the ego are transferred to group life. He now addresses a new objection to having individual psychology, a problem he will meet by analyzing resistance to narration. Freud proposes that to represent the mythology of group psychology, one must respond with narrative revolts. His best advice is that we put group psychology into words.

What forms do these narrative revolts take? Psychoanalytic concepts are made from unsolved problems and, for Freud, the most unsolvable one concerns the question of origin or an ontology of psychology. This ontology forms the subtext, but not the cause, of the child's Oedipal question, the destabilizing tendency of the uncanny, the problem of the repressed and its return and, in this chapter, the poesies of the group's libidinal ties. Before natality, before the infantile, before psychology, before time itself, Freud will relate the development of groups to the mythic histrionics of the primal horde, another representation that will bring him to the origins of symbolization that he roots in a story created by a poet. Through myths, he creates the ontology of imagination and then discusses what is unreal about reality. Our purpose will be to pressure educational life with Freud's new questions. In brief, our approach will not be to ask how groups can be better handled. Instead, we ask prior questions: what can be said about the inner world in a study of group psychology? What does love have to do with group psychology?

Freud's challenge is to read group psychology through the dynamic unconscious and its drives. These are psychoanalytic constructions needed to narrate the procedures of sexuality, repression, and representation. One of the most astute and imaginative readers of Freudian thought, Julia Kristeva, presents Freud's method as constituting "narrative revolts," a style of thinking that permits psychoanalysis "to access the archaic, to overturn conscious meaning" (2000, p. 15). In considering group psychology through its dynamics of objections, objects, and obstacles, Freud is then able to imagine ethical projects for the thinking subject: working through and sublimation. A revolution for conscious meaning permits us to speculate on the return of the repressed and present cultural life as subject to the composition and decomposition of psychical reality and its conflicts.

The narrative revolt Freud proposes, however, is not so much a story of group psychology's inability to know its own psychical acts as it is an argument for the ego's audacity to narrate its own work of thought, comment on what it is like to be with others and to be like others, and find a separate and distinctive self. The narrative Freud creates then is psychoanalytical because it binds imagination, language, and fantasy to affects, symptoms, and defenses. Group psychology becomes a story about trying to tell a story of history, one where cul-de-sacs, conflicts, losses, and libidinal strivings adhere to ideals and where worldviews stifle meaning. As for the force of the uncanny in this little book, Freud is beholden to mythology. Literary life is exemplary material to expand psychoanalysis into an allegory on social love and hate.

"Group psychology" picks up the discarded threads of his earlier work and weaves their significance into something new and startling: an analysis of the ego through the problem of belonging and separation. This may be what he means by the conflict between regard and disregard for real relations with others. Throughout his work, and, as one may surmise, in conflictive terms, Freud posits the complexity, motility, and transcriptions of the ego: as relative to its own psychical poesies; as libidinal and anxious; as a love object; as a protective, dependent, and defensive creature; as partially unconscious; as closest to the world but never so far away from its own wishes; as affected by time, language, and negation; as a fight between ideas and affect and between pleasure and reality; as adaptive, partial, and subject to its own splitting; as subject to narcissist injury, the weight of meaning, and feelings of unification; as a bodily surface and its own projection; and as an organization. His study on group psychology extends his understanding of the ego into a world of egos, now subject to affecting one another, to hostility and rivalry, to demands for love and justice, and to internalizing ego ideals. With group psychology the ego becomes inter-subjective and intra-psychical, additional elements required for myth making and narrative revolts.

Here, too, Freud brings into the fray two of the most difficult and resisted ideas of psychoanalysis—the unconscious and sexuality—as affecting and structuring the object cathexis of group life that is then transformed into introjected ego processes. His analysis of the ego in the group brings new problems to the question of transference. Libidinality and sexuality are taken through the urgency of emotional ties, themselves fashioned from an earlier ego defense: identifications. The ego will become the sum of its identifications. However, things will not add up. In their dictionary entry on "the ego," Laplanche and Pontalis (1973) stress the ambiguity of this concept and its affecting terms: "Identification is now more than the mere expression of a relationship between myself and another person, while the ego may now undergo radical changes because of it, becoming the intrasubjective residue of an intersubjective relation" (p. 137). A great deal is held together in this formulation. By placing within the ego an imaginary intercourse with relics of its earliest libidinal relations, Freud is proposing to narrate a story of how the ego affects its own design and, with the advent of love, its interest in thinking.

Freud's analysis of the ego permits a new understanding of the unconscious and sexuality, themselves obstacles to and resources for ego processes such as sublimation, thinking, and narrative, all reposes for bodily action. Somewhat surprisingly, he will posit group psychology as made from an uncanny love. It is as if, for the ego, there is always group psychology. Just as Freud has expanded the meanings of sexuality into a story of forgotten origin, involuntary passions, and aggressive drives, he extends the ontology of individual psychology with the mythology and poetics of object group life.

In his contemporary discussion of Freud's "Group psychology," John Kerr (2001) describes how frustrating it is to read: the text is a labyrinth, and readers are apt to get lost in Freud's many asides. Further, the book turns reading into an experiment with meaning. Though no direct route stands between Freud's words and our meanings—and indeed, Freud approached meaning through its sliding capacity for ambiguity, indefiniteness, and ambivalence—Kerr recommends that the text be read clinically, as a story of symptoms and libidinal ties and as psychology calling for interpretation. On the manifest level, the problem appears two-sided: what keeps groups together and why do they fall apart? However, then the problem grows murky and latent as Freud attempts to situate the origin of psychology itself and so must construct what is most archaic, repressed, and forgotten. If we read Freud's text clinically, we can come to the idea that, first of all, there is something that is not group psychology but nonetheless involves feelings toward the group. Second, we might then begin to wonder whether the individual already anticipates and so projects group psychology into any group life. This uncanny factor, an alienation or collapse of feelings with the unknown situations, leads Freud to reconsider the ego's history of love. This turn leaves the clinic and boldly enters the literary world of mythology dedicated to representing the destiny of emotional life.

Consideration of group life lends new psychical tasks to the ego: the need to work through its attraction to authority, to the past, to the impulsions of its own unconscious drives, and to the pull of narcissism of minor differences. The book is composed of 12 short chapters and then a postscript that may almost be read as if it belonged to another article. The postscript raises one of the most surprising claims for why narrative revolts are a tonic to both group psychology and the analysis of the ego. Freud does throw down the gauntlet: he sees in the group formation elements of primal hordes, archaic object relations, the return of the primal father in the person of the leader, the repetition compulsion, the Oedipal complex, and archaic feelings of envy, jealousy, hostility, and panic over the loss of love. From this history of negativity, operating within any identification, there will also be the reasons and materials for sublimation, creativity, and ego ideals. Essentially, it is through group psychology that Freud will develop his theory of object relations and soon after, with his "The Ego and the Id" (1923a), transform the psychical apparatus into agencies with a third dynamic mediator: the superego, a reservoir of conscience, self-criticism, moral anxiety, object cathexes and identifications, and an unconscious record of Oedipal strivings and cultural prohibitions.

Explorations into group psychology are also an occasion for Freud to return to his earlier interest in hypnosis and thought transference and to comment on popular theories of his time, such as the herd instinct, hysterical contagion, imitation, and mob psychology. The prevailing belief he dissected, and one that still holds currency today, is that groups make the individual into a compliant, hostile follower led by exaggerated affect mistaken for ideas and subject members to the defense of altruistic surrender and vicarious living. Why one might give up one's own mind brought Freud to question individual psychology. As for the texts of Freud's time that addressed group living, he did not consider them psychological. For Freud, psychology was a question of emotional history that unconsciously orients the libidinal conflicts of consciousness and every one of its concepts of apperception and attention that give the world notice. In this sense, psychology is always a psychology of love and, therefore, must struggle with its own meanings, reasoning, and losses. Love will be our greatest unsolved problem. As Freud tries to understand what is so maddening about conceptualizing group psychology, he learns something new about the ego's relation to itself. Psychology has arrived.

The questions Freud raised remain pertinent. How do groups create their libidinal ties? Are these emotional ties made from suggestion, as with hypnosis; contagion, as with panic; or, fascination and attraction, as with sexuality? In what ways do emotional ties and the mental constellations that carry them affect not only one's capacity to think, judge, and reality test but service the arts and crafts of individuality? Is group psychology, beginning in dyadic relations, older than individual psychology? Where do the group's ideals come from? Does a group make a leader, or is it the other way around? What does being a follower cost? What counts as group psychology if what also counts are the unconscious and sexuality? Finally, can group psychology be psychoanalyzed, or is it that psychoanalysis may now consider differently its own views about the advent of the ego and its fragile narcissism?

At the very least, Freud is reorienting his ongoing existential questions: what can be said about psychological life, and how does the outside world proposition the subject's interiority? Without taking into account the psychology of group, he wrote, his own view of the individual is incomplete and

> presents the surprising fact that under a certain condition this individual, whom it had come to understand, thought, felt and acted

in quite a different way from what would have been expected. And this condition is his insertion into a collection of people which has acquired the characteristic of a 'psychological group'.

(1921, p. 72)

What Freud expected was more like what he hoped for: that individuals would not be carried away by the demands, fantasies, and illusions of group psychology *and* that there could be something called a *thinking group*.

The problem, however, as Freud admits in the opening epigraph, is that there is hardly a time when the individual is without some sort of group, the earliest ones being the family and then with institutions of education. Yet, these childhood groups, our earliest emotional ties, are also repressed relics that return to both ward off conflict and animate our ambivalence about being with others. So, one part of this text's strangeness has to do with the ways Freud deals with the unexpected: or the return of this repressed. The repressed that returns is one of prehistory, what has been called *archaic*: the terror and bellicose tragedy of ancient Greek mythology wherein characters act without knowing their intentions, where Eros is blind, where learning always occurs too late, and where protagonists can never return to their origins (Spitz, 1994). This psychoanalytic situation involves the dynamic unconscious: inchoate impressions; strains of forgotten histories of learning for love; fragments of archaic fantasies of education; and flashes of omnipotent thought, hostile impulses, and drive impulsions. Sexuality itself is now extended; its origin is modeled on the other and its force modeled on the drive.

However, we should also admit that Freud was no stranger to the conflict of group psychology. One might wonder about the 65-year-old Freud's motives for its writing. In this sense, the text can also be analyzed as a piece of transference with his psychoanalytic group. Though Freud's vast archive of letters serves as one indicator for the inherent conflicts psychoanalysis posed, his (1914a) admittedly subjective early history of the psychoanalytic movement comments on internal arguments and his separation from such analysts as Jung and Adler. This approach personalizes history and would bring us to analyze Freud's friendships, his talent for gathering enemies, his wishes for the psychoanalytic movement and, as some would see it, his megalomania.

To go even further, this 1921 study of groups could be read as a commentary on the psychoanalytic movement at the height of conflict and diversity: the establishment of a secret committee, intrigues over leadership, and the eschewing fights over the status, directions, and theories of the new field of child psychoanalysis and education. The text, too, could also be situated within the larger social/political theater as it comes after the demise of the Austria-Hungarian Empire, the defeat of Germany in World War I, and the growth of fascism in Germany and Italy and socialism in Russia and Hungary. Surely Freud's thinking about war brought him to try to understand the seeds of hostility.

Yet, to take this little book in its own right, to read for its literary qualities—its gaps, silences, hints, broken off thoughts, and mythology—and so to read more like a poet than a social scientist, a clinician, or an historian would be to see why Freud anchors group psychology in the unconscious conflicts of love caught between the internal and external world. A literary approach would allow us to see what resists history and what cannot be history. It also brings the problem of ethics because, unless the past can be understood as placed in time, unless we can begin to understand why putting events into time creates narratives testifying to loss that paradoxically permit greater psychological freedom, the subject will be under the sway of the unconscious, itself timeless. The issue that group psychology brought to the fore is that external events are registrations without awareness. These include the impressive fantasies of infantile reality and the uncanny urge of the transference of internal compulsions onto perceptions and acting out.

Again, the text itself is uncanny, filled with mythic, fantastical things such as the primal horde, the son's taboo against looking the primal father in the eyes, hypnosis, and then, something terribly ordinary: an exchange of obedience for love. Something is scary and familiar about this archaic heritage of group psychology and the ways in which it is conveyed and introjected. With a literary approach, the text can also be read as allegory: an imaginative experiment in narrating the ordinary conflicts of classroom life by giving an account of an unconscious story of education that flowers in the compost heap of group psychology.

THE UNCANNY

Freud (1919c) had taken on the topic of frightening feelings in "The Uncanny" (*unheimlich*), a literary study that can be read as anticipating the subterranean depths of group psychology. Things that feel uncanny are strangely familiar, uncomfortable, disorienting, difficult to place, rather mesmerizing, and misleading. The uncanny is an index of mistaken vision that lends to accidents and estranging coincidences an odd sense of familiarly. It confuses the ego's confidence in interpreting reality and disregards its real relations to others. Uncanny feelings confirm ideas felt as long ago discarded. The simplest things (sudden sounds, words, images, and inanimate objects such as dolls, puppets, and stuffed animals, for instance) are experienced as if reminiscent of other scenes of fright, fear, and anxiety.

In his paper on the uncanny, Freud examines etymology, wherein he considers the relation between the words *home* and *estrangement* and then brings into this mix a discourse on aesthetics. Much of this paper is taken up by a long description of E. T. A. Hoffmann's (1816) short story, "The Sandman." This fairy tale figure, sometimes terrifying and sometimes soothing, is known for placing sand in the eyes of children to put them to sleep. Proof of the sandman's visit is a crust caught in the eyes and that causes difficulty upon opening them. The wish to sleep is disturbed by the sudden anxiety of not being able to wake up.

Hoffmann's tale, one of uncertainty, mistaken identity, fear, and horror, concerns a protagonist who confuses one unknown person with a terrifying other. The protagonist, caught in the collapse of his feelings with situations that are not his feelings, is uncertain as to whether this unknown person is a stranger, a benefactor, or a murderer. This uncertainty, which sounds suspiciously like the Oedipal myth, leads the story to its tragic conclusion. The protagonist has lost control of meaning and quickly descends into madness, attempted murder, then suicide.

From Hoffmann's tale, Freud speculated on the child's fear of losing sight and tied this to fears of castration, or separation from what is loved. The uncanny feelings pertain to an unconscious compulsion to repeat earlier repressed infantile impressions. As the essay is about to conclude, Freud rehearses objections to his idea that uncanny feelings harken back to something familiar or the return of the repressed. He takes as his last example the adult's capacity to be overtaken by childhood fears, anxiety animated by the hearing of strange noises, or experiencing a weird coincidence: "Concerning the factors of silence, solitude and darkness, we can only say that they are actually elements in the production of the infantile anxiety from which the majority of human beings have never become quite free" (1919c, p. 252).

Never becoming "quite free" is the leitmotif of Freud's "Group psychology." However, we need to ask, free from what? This question will lead to a reconsideration of the compulsions of education—itself a scene of group psychology—and allow us to clarify two of the most difficult concepts (as objection object, and obstacle) Freud presents: the unconscious and sexuality. Between these poles, Freud will situate our fragile psychological freedom but as at odds with its own desire. Let us return to this strange text and ask again: what happens in group psychology?

"A RANGE OF PHENOMENON"

Freud's opening problem is this: how does the group exert its influence over its members? Le Bon's *Psychologie des foules* serves as his foil. He quotes liberally from this influential book, interrupting his description by noting what Le Bon has left out. Le Bon's explanation is that individuals give their independent minds over to the prestige of a leader, almost as if they were hypnotized and so led by the immediacy of the unconscious, itself subject to magical thinking, omnipotent wishes, and persuaded by myths. Yet, Freud raises the objection: why would an individual regress to earlier infantile modes of being? Freud also objects to his second source, McDougall's *Group Mind*. This study stressed how, within group psychology, there is an intensification of emotion and a lowering of intellect. What takes over are contagion, imitation, and suggestibility. However, rather than becoming concerned with mechanisms of compliance, as McDougall stressed, Freud takes another road. In wondering about the psychological significance of becoming affected, he turns to libido theory and the poet's song:

> We call by that name the energy, regarded as a quantitative magnitude (though not at present actually measurable), of those instincts which have to do with all that may be compromised under the word "love." The nucleus of what we mean by love naturally consists (and this is what is commonly called love, and what the poets sing of) in sexual love with sexual union as its aim. But we do not separate from this— what in any case has a share in the name "love"—on the one hand,

self-love, and on the other, love for parents and children, friendship and love for humanity in general, and also devotion to concrete objects and to abstract ideas ... .All these tendencies are an expression of the same instinctual impulses ... in other circumstances they are diverted from this aim or are prevented from reaching it, though always preserving enough of their original nature to keep their identity recognizable (as in such features as the longing for proximity, and self-sacrifice.

(1921, pp. 90–91)

Essentially, Freud understands group psychology through the problem of love, a representative, force, consequence, and function, however sublimated, of sexuality. It is here that Freud leaves his own objections and addresses those of his readers. Love, even the most innocent type between parents and children, includes an unconscious sexual foundation: "We are of the opinion, then, that language has carried out an entirely justifiable piece of unification in creating the word 'love' with its numerous uses ... [And psychoanalysis] has done nothing original in taking love in this 'wider' sense" (p. 91).

Yet this "wider" sense is precisely where the objections, objects, and obstacles begin because the vicissitudes of sexuality bring into question every motive for attachment, interest, ideals, concepts, and wish, including those we cannot imagine as originally sexual. Without broadening the meaning of sexuality, that is, without extending sexuality beyond biology and into psychology and cultural life (and the word *love*, Freud already argued, does this work), he would be hard-pressed to even posit the emotional valance of groups or attempt exploration into their irrationality. Further objections follow. If the aim of sexuality is diverted, does that not mean that the object and source are now irrelevant? Or, why still insist that any emotional tie leans upon sexuality at all? Freud responds to his objector:

Psycho-analysis ... gives these love instincts the name of sexual instincts, a postiori and by reason of their origin. The majority of "educated" people have regarded this nomenclature as an insult, and have taken their revenge by retorting upon psycho-analysis with the reproach of "pan-sexualism." Anyone who considers sex as something mortifying and humiliating to human nature is at liberty to make use of the more genteel expressions "Eros" and "erotic." I might have done so myself from the first and thus have spared myself much opposition. But I did not want to, for I like to avoid concessions to faintheartedness. One can never tell where that road may lead one; one gives way first in words, and then little by little in substance too. I cannot see any merit in being ashamed of sex.

(p. 91)

The issue is that love is as much the basis of group psychology as it is of individual psychology. Love holds groups together and is the reason for feelings of wanting to belong. In positing a psychology of love and in attending to what is most difficult about its claims, Freud departs from Le Bon, McDougall, and his detractors. Indeed, by the fourth chapter of his little book, once Freud has taken apart the logic of his predecessors, showed how the individual is social from the beginning of life and, therefore, does not need to come equipped with a "herd instinct," he dedicates the rest of the text to the idea that love, a great unifier and source of ambivalence, sutures groups.

THE DRIVES

Again we break our discussion for brief comments on the drives and their destiny. We need to reintroduce them to understand the emotional force of Freud's psychology of love and this key insistence: that group psychology is oriented by the motive of love, disoriented by its loss, inhibited in aim by identifications, and subject to the glamour of leaders.

The idea of the drive (*Trieb*) is one of Freud's more difficult postulates. It undergirds his views of sexuality, the struggle for life and death, and the problem of pleasure and unpleasure. The difficulty is two fold. One part is with the ambiguity of the notion of drive, itself a way to conceptualize internal stimulation and tension that seek release. Freud thought of the drives as pushes and, through psychology, as psychical representatives of somatic processes. The other difficulty is with their indeterminacy: the drives are thought to be the means for psychical reality to exhale pleasure and unpleasure. Indeed, when Freud wrote his papers on metapsychology, he proposed the drive as

> a concept on the frontier between the mental and the somatic, as the psychical representative of the stimuli originating from within the organism and reaching the mind, as a measure of the demand made upon the mind for work in consequence of its connection with the body.
>
> (1915a, p. 122)

Freud understood the drive through its qualities and quantities: the drive is thought to have a pressure [*Drang*], an aim [*Ziel*], an object [*Objekt*], and a source [*Ouelle*]. At the time of the metapsychology, Freud had two drives in mind—the sexual drive and the self-preservation drive. With this early view, sexuality is greatly dispersed, polymorphous, and perverse, as it was described in his 1905 "Three Essays on Sexuality." There is no natural progression among pressure, modes of release, and choice of object, although these elements may constitute styles of loving made from the accumulated force of individual history and the ways an individual was initially loved from infancy onward.

Freud also describes the drive through its qualities of transformations: "reversal into its opposite, turning round upon the subject's own self, repression, and sublimation ... . Reversal of an instinct into its opposite resolves on closer examination into two different processes: a change from activity to passivity, and a reversal of its content" (1915a, pp. 126–127). As for psychology, only one drive can turn into its opposite—love into hate—and hate, Freud thought, was older than love. We will see this insistence return when Freud grapples with the origin of groups. In this early formulation, however, Freud thought of two drives: sexuality and self-preservation.

A year prior to his publication on group psychology, in "Beyond the Pleasure Principle," Freud (1920a) would change this to the postulates of Eros and Thanatos, or the life drive and the death drive. Their work and motility would now concern binding or creating greater unities (the life drive), and unbinding, or destroying, reducing, and reverting back to earliest forms (the death drive). Their indeterminacy would be discussed through the problem of anxiety and loss. In his "New Introductory Lectures," their impertinency becomes noted: "The theory of the instincts is so to say our mythology. Instincts are mythical entities, magnificent in their indefiniteness. In our work we cannot for a moment disregard them, yet we are never sure that we are seeing them clearly" (1933, p. 95).

Readers should keep this problem in mind: the drives are mythology and serve that function. They are a story of origins without memory and words and the means to tell the story. We can now return to this paradox of mythology as representing the unrepresentable and consider it as what founds group psychology.

"A COMPANY OF PORCUPINES"

By chapter six, after Freud has given examples of two artificial groups, the Church and the army, he turns to the individual's emotional nature through a parable: "According to Schopenhauer's famous simile of the freezing porcupines no one can tolerate a too intimate approach to his neighbour" (1921, p. 101). When these freezing animals huddle for warmth, the pain of their quills repels them. As for humans, there is no emotional relationship that does not contain elements of hostility and ambivalence, the pain of being touched, and anxiety over separation. In the porcupine parable, Freud sees the seeds of self-love or narcissism and the hostility that emerges when individuals feel an obstacle to desire or when they feel they must somehow change something about themselves in order to be with others. Groups, Freud suggests, limit narcissism: "Love for oneself knows only one barrier— love for others, love for objects" (102). There are, in groups, new libidinal ties or what Freud calls, "love instincts which have been diverted from their original aims, though they do not operate with less energy on that account" (p. 103). This new form of love is how Freud describes *identifications*, the subject of his longest chapter.

Identifications are the earliest form of emotional ties. It is how the world is taken inside. To show how these ties are formed, Freud turns to a discussion of the Oedipal complex, or the triadic family structure, as the first group psychology, replete with passionate conflicts of love, hate, jealously, and ambivalence. Like Sophocles's tragedy, *Oedipus Tyrannos*, passions have free reign, are acted out without knowledge of consequence or without psychological significance, and these feeling events cannot be narrated.

Freud dated the Oedipal complex in children between the ages of three through five, when they are already involved in language and symbolism, when they want to know their story of origin but have their own sexual theories, and when they are able to put their demands, questions, and theories of the world into words directed to their parents. This is the parents' uncanny scene. The child falls in love with one parent and considers the other an obstacle. It is a time when the child first experiences the entwining of love, hate, and ambivalence, contrary feelings attaching to the same object. With latency, this period of intense desire undergoes repression, and the child can then turn to the world of other children, collect new objects, and form new ties, themselves resources for knowledge and identity and for belonging and separation.

Two different types of emotional ties are made through the Oedipal dilemma, and it is here that Freud posits the beginning of group psychology. One parent may serve as the model for the child's future and, therefore, stays in the realm of identifications, whereas the other parent serves as the child's fantasies for a timeless present, becoming what Freud called the *choice of an object*. Through identification, the qualities of both the loved and hated object become the raw material for character, whereas with object choice, one wishes to have, rather than be, the other, and it serves as the raw material for sexuality's psychology. These emotional ties are unconscious wishes, and Freud is at great pains to stress that the status of love in the poesies of the self is unconscious in its effects and destiny. As fantasies of experience and as an ego defense, identifications are not yet a story as Oedipal love is impossible, forbidden, and then forgotten or repressed.

Identifications, or emotional ties, are the means for the ego to create, project, and attach to the external world of others. The psychology Freud constructs, because it leans on love, is without boundary. Projection and introjection alter the ego's design. As libidinal attachments, they evolve into sympathy and empathy but also, when disappointed, carry their potential: paranoia and hostility. The problem for the child is that "the model" one would like to become turns into an obstacle and is met by the child's objections. The "model object" gets in the way of the child's libidinal fantasy. This allows Freud to speculate on the qualities of identifications: they are partial, unconscious, and ambivalent:

> Identification, in fact, is ambivalent from the very first; it can turn into an expression of tenderness as easily as into a wish for someone's removal. It behaves like a derivative of the first, *oral* phase of the organization of libido, in which the object that we long for and prize is assimilated by eating and is in that way annihilated as such.
>
> (1921, p. 105)

Identification, then, is a conceptual turn in Freud's vocabulary and covers a great deal of territory, beginning with the creation of the ego and the ego ideal. Its various themes are composed from ego defenses that are also a libidinal aim-inhibited mechanism of psychical life, and defenses sustain an unconscious equation of love with aggression and hostility, as identifications are also ambivalent. As with all of Freud's psychoanalytic objects of knowledge, identification will take its strength through its great plasticity and capaciousness. Identifications can also be taken back into the ego, causing a regression to an earlier state, to melancholia, and to isolation.

Slowly, Freud will relate these erotic Oedipal ties as the basis of group psychology. Before that, he takes another detour in his eighth chapter, "Being in love and hypnosis." Again, he reminds his readers of the vast geography the term *love* covers, owing, he thought, to an original quality of sexuality, namely its polymorphous perversity. Love is the only word that can transform from sexual desire to affection and be used to signify love of ideas and abstractions. Freud considers repression, or the severing of the affect from the idea, as responsible for meaning's transformations but also insists that language itself has these properties through euphemism, generality, and irony. As for the waning of Oedipal desire, with repression there is no final goodbye: "It is well known that the earlier 'sensual' tendencies remain more or less strongly preserved in the unconscious, so that in a certain sense the whole of the original current continues to exist" (1921, p. 111).

What repression leaves in its wake is a new relation to the old emotional tie: idealization, or a transformation of narcissism and its remnant found in the tendency to over-value the object, exaggerate its qualities, and generally bestow on it all modes of devotion and self sacrifice. This, too, will be an unrequited love crusting over Oedipal longings preserved in the unconscious. Identifications are the remnants of sexuality, and Freud then creates a

> formula for the libidinal constitution of groups ... those that have a leader and have not been able by means of too much "organization" to acquire secondarily the characteristics of an individual. *A primary group of this kind is a number of individuals who have put one and the same object in the place of their ego idea and have consequently identified themselves with one another in their ego.*
>
> (1921, p. 116; ital. orig.)

Group psychology is as much an internal affair as it is an external organization.

SOCIAL SPIRIT AND PRIMARY HORDES

It can certainly seem as if group psychology is a repetition of Oedipal struggles, dashed hopes, and then compromises made. All these uncanny experiences are a part of the group psychology, but its original conflict, namely a struggle for love, from Freud's telling, never quite disappears. A rough kernel of resentment and hostility survives, and the superego, the sum of identifications with parental love and cultural prohibitions, testifies in the form of the ego's guilt at not measuring up.

The issue, again, is the sexual foundation of any group; Eros is needed for identifications to emerge, but Eros, that great fickle unifier, shoots his arrows with blindness. This may be why Freud placed being in love side by side with the idea of hypnosis, of giving the self over to another authority's influence. Yet by his ninth chapter, he dismisses the view that individuals are subject to "a herd instinct" or can be mindlessly led without excising their reasoning. Freud reminds the reader that children will not follow everyone and, indeed, want their parents close by. It takes time for children to experience group feeling, and only when they are sent to school does the idea of the group become a new psychological reality. Until then, and in the family scene, there is competition (whether real or imaginary) among individual children. Younger children envy older children's freedom, and older children feel jealousy toward the attention parents bestow on the newly born. We have seen this hostility before in the child's Oedipal wishes to be the parent's only one. However, it is parents and, once in school, other children who break up this fantasy. The original hostility of identifications returns in the structure of school life:

> So there grows up in the troop of children a communal or group feeling, which is then further developed at school. The first demand made by this reaction-formation is for justice, for equal treatment for all. We all know how loudly and implacably this claim is put forward at school. If one cannot be the favourite oneself, at all events nobody else shall be the favourite.
>
> (1921, p. 120)

Even in our most altruistic demands for social justice, Freud finds traces of sexuality and an original repressed hostility wherein equal treatment can quickly transform into punishment for all. No human cry is immune from the force and indeed trauma of its prehistory, and the unconscious is that testimony to a time before meaning and where passions rule. In his understanding of group psychology, the unconscious is as fundamental to consciousness as it is a force of its collapse. Whereas school life may give the reader a real example of these unconscious events, with his next chapter the reader is again plunged into mythology and its cycles of repetitive violence, passion, and struggles against fate. The idea of origin will take shape through fantasy.

His chapter titled "The group and the primal horde" begins, "In 1912 I took up a conjecture of Darwin's to the effect that the primitive form of human society was that of a horde ruled over despotically by a powerful male" (1921, p. 122). Freud is referring to his earlier book, "Totem and Taboo," wherein he first speculated on the myth of the primal horde, a band of brothers agitated by sexual jealousy toward the father that leads them to murder him. Then, in their guilt, they establish laws and prohibitions against incest. With the myth of totem and taboo, Freud finds a way to represent the movement from drives to representation. When sexuality can be represented, culture can be created.

His theory of group psychology leans on this myth, first as a way into arguing that group psychology is older than individual psychology and then to consider the uncanny power of the leader in groups:

> The uncanny and coercive characteristics of group formations, which are shown in the phenomena of suggestion that accompany them, may therefore with justice be traced back to the fact of their origin from the primal horde. The leader of the group is still the dreaded primal father; the group still wishes to be governed by unrestricted force; it has an extreme passion for authority … a conviction which is not based upon perception and reasoning but upon an erotic tie.
>
> (1921, pp. 127–128)

The group ideal, introjected as an ego ideal, is made from shared feelings for the leader but now substitutes for the individual's ego. Emotional ties are incredibly uncanny. Essentially, through the violent myth of the primal horde and the primal father, Freud posits the pressures and regressions of group psychology as "an extreme passion for authority" (ibid).

If taken as *telos*, the myth of the primal horde has the capacity to diminish all hints of the individual's emergence, all hints of objections, and seems to replace the subject with the object. Almost counter-intuitively, Freud is trying to analyze the ego as a precipice of group psychology and its archaic history. The group that he will slowly end his book with, however, is an internal one: its form will be the conflict among the unconscious, the ego, and the ego ideals. No longer a thing in itself, group psychology becomes an uncanny object relation of interiority and thus inaugurates a new origin: the psychological self.

"SIDE PATHS"

Freud concludes with a postscript: "side paths which we avoided pursuing in the first instance but in which there was much that offered us promises of insight" (1921, p. 134). He picks up the threads of unsolvable problems with "the advance of the imagination" (p. 136). Further, he suggests some approaches to understanding the early question of the exceptional conditions that individual psychology creates to disregard real relations with others. As well, his postscript considers how psychology can represent ontology, or a story of origins needed to enter into human history. The paradox is that he will draw upon a narrative that is not history at all but that nonetheless urges us into history.

In the postscript, Freud writes sparingly of sublimation, a psychoanalytic object relation to knowledge given to the ego to create, from the sexual drive, erotic or sublime representations that are directed by desire, invite deep attachments, and require subjectivity. Within this process of creation, in the imagination, the ego's freedom may disregard relations to others. One might argue that Freud's book on group psychology is a strong model of imagination: He brings incompatible ideas into every page and essentially accepts that this may hurt the reader's feelings.

However, another model is education. Sublimation as an unsolved problem is what the ego carries over to it. Yet sublimation cannot be taught even as education relies upon the individual's interest in transforming internal conflicts into symbolization. It is also where education founders when it mindlessly repeats idealizations of cooperative learning, role models, and socialization. One of the implicit tensions these approaches to emotional ties bury is that individuals are educated in groups but urged to think for the self, to create one's own mind, and to overcome the fear, prejudice, and acting out that suture group life but destroy the capacity to think. Yet, the dominant and taken-for-granted discourse on learning only magnifies one aspect of this world: that students should behave and that identifications are only conscious.

A psychoanalytic account of group psychology gives us some additional dilemmas. From a Freudian perspective, the educator's demand that the student delay gratification for the work of learning is both necessary and aggravating: necessary, because education requires that we tell time, grapple with morality, and feel guilt; and aggravating, because on the one side, real relations to others have to be disregarded and, on the other side, becoming a subject with others means narrating one's life and coming into conflict with representations and abstractions greater than what experience provides. Education, for Freud, is the ego's second chance. The ego's movement, however, is from group psychology to individual psychology. Education's progression can be seen in similar terms. Its practices must exceed temptations toward normalization and standardization that group psychology also demands. If education is to be more than uncanny or frighteningly familiar, both normalization and standardization need to be understood as problems of narratives, not facts. If these social constraints and modes of docility can be treated as an object to ponder rather than a reality to impose or even to follow, the character of education can transform.

In a flight of fantasy, Freud's postscript gives us a clue as to why he brought into discussion so many myths to describe our emotional world, why he was so preoccupied with what confines the mind, and why he began a story of individual psychology with that of a group:

> It was then, perhaps, that some individual, in the exigency of his longing, may have been moved to free himself from the group and take over the father's part. He who did this was the first epic poet; and the advance was achieved in his imagination. This poet disguised the truth with lies in accordance with his longing. He invented the heroic myth ... . The myth, then, is the step by which the individual emerges from group psychology ... .The poet who had taken this step and had in this way set himself free from the group in his imagination, is nevertheless able ... to find his way back to reality. For he goes and relates to the group his hero's deeds which he has invented. At bottom this hero is no one but himself. Thus he lowers himself to the level of reality and raises his hearers to the level of imagination.
>
> (1921, pp. 136–137)

The ego's paradox is that it is already in the world and must find a way to live there. The poet's solution is narrative revolts, an appeal to the imagination. The poet constructs an affecting story, one wherein people can see themselves anew and think about their quills. The poet revolts against the suspension of meaning that group psychology also creates by giving representation to that uncanny suspension and, in doing so, must disregard real relations to others.

Here is where Freud may be grappling with education's pleasure-and-reality principle and raising the question of whether education can exceed the uncanny Oedipal crisis it also leans upon. So, the big question is how from identifications with group psychology narrative revolts can occur. Freud may be read as suggesting that in education, identifications or emotional ties of group psychology need to be sublimated and given over to the transformation of the figural. Here is where the acquisition of literacy overturns consciousness by joining imagination to its own capacity for symbolization. The great question is whether the conditions of education, for any age, can provoke more than the return of an original hostility and so break open unconscious mythology that equates learning with both the need for an authority and the desire to be punished. Can the educator and student take on the poet's responsibility and narrate the force of education and its group psychology? The analysis of the ego is, after all, a work of language. This begins with the poet's call for poetic license, narrative revolts, and poetic justice.

5

"WILD" EDUCATION: SEE UNDER *UNSOLVED PROBLEMS OF*

(5) *Education* can be described without more ado as an incitement to the conquest of the pleasure principle, and to its replacement by the reality principle; it seeks, that is, to lend its help to the developmental process which affects the ego. To this end it makes use of an offer of love as a reward from the educators; and it therefore fails if a spoilt child thinks that it possesses that love in any case and cannot lose it whatever happens.

(8) The strangest characteristic of unconscious (repressed) processes, to which no investigator can become accustomed without the exercise of great self-discipline, is due to their entire disregard of reality-testing; they equate reality of thoughts with external actuality, and wishes with their fulfillment—with the event—just as happens automatically under the dominance of the ancient pleasure principle.

—Sigmund Freud, "Two principles of mental functioning"

THINKING PROBLEMS

The preceding notes conclude Freud's (1911) speculative sketch on the pleasure principle and the reality principle; both propose the psyche's radicalism. These remarks follow on the trail of his dream theory; they carry the force of the elemental wish and its "wild education" into the swirls of the mind and then outward into the world of others. Notice, however, in Freud's aforementioned point five, that it may take a modern army of teachers to disillusion "the ancient pleasure principle." Later in this chapter, we turn to the thickets of the teacher's pleasure principle, her or his infantile roots of wild education. For now, we observe that Freud thought of the teacher's responsibility as receiving wishes and interpreting them. Teachers cannot work from their automatic pilot; they have the added burden of overruling the dispensation of unconditional love. With rewards come punishments, and the greatest is disappointed love. However, students, after all, are no strangers to these events because rewards and punishments also occur in the mind.

If it now seems as though education is only an intractable battle of conquest and defeat, and sometimes it does feel that way with our contemporary mania for success and failure, Freud proposes an analysis of this objection. Though no stranger to resistances to psychoanalysis, with the question of education he looks inward, to what resists within his own theory. With a careful reading of this 1911 paper on mental functioning, our focus begins with the question of why Freud must grapple with a new psychoanalytic problem. He writes this as one of "bringing psychological significance of the real external world into the structure of our theories" (p. 218). The idea of psychological significance carries unstated difficulties: significance is notoriously elusive, personal, and fragile and, while impervious to outside instructions, depends upon making meaning, or constructing relations to the external world. However, psychological significance is also a new enigmatic object for theory and is easily lost in the child's unanswerable question that begins with the word *why*? Theory itself must bow to this great problem and be affected by it. Though in the previous chapter we proposed Freud's struggle to bring psychoanalysis into the world of group psychology to learn more about the ego, here we present his engagement with bringing the world of psychological significance into psychoanalytic theory. Educational theory, we argue, must be as bold.

We want to bring these unsolved problems of reality, pleasure, and theory into the pedagogical world and ask, what can psychological significance mean to the wishful mind? How does bestowing the bountiful meaning of psychoanalysis affect the ways education can be represented and interpreted? Throughout this 1911 article, Freud implies that making the world meaningful is what makes up the mind and that meaning emerges from estrangement: the self must learn to think about its mental acts, lend them psychological meaning, and oppose its own temptations of being swept away by the haphazardness and impulsiveness of its unconscious wishes. However, the self must lean upon these wishes to think and imagine. This conflict is the ego's plight and potential for learning. We will also consider education as having a comparable struggle; it, too, must delay immediate gratification, grapple with significance, and trade in uncertainty. However, only with regard for psychological significance can Freud craft psychoanalysis into a new ethic for the work of learning. Education, we argue, must find its ways in this uncharted path. The road will be bumpy.

Our approach to Freud's dilemma of thinking education will also be wild, breaking open his chronology with his and our narrative revolts. The large problem is with education's development and how it is affected by beginnings and the world that also revises its conflicts. This tack follows on the heels of what Freud set in motion: the force of education proceeds along the lines of deferred action; over the course of Freud's writing, there are seismic shifts in the tectonic plates of psychoanalytic knowledge that unsettle his previous views; and his writing conceptualizes resistance to learning through the construct of infantile amnesia, or what is buried by the unconscious and preserved there. His style of thinking can be read as culminating in this paradox: education as an unsolved problem. In this final chapter, we will have to reconstruct a Freudian approach to education through a rearrangement of his work, interrupting Freud's 1911 article on the two principles of mental functioning with his metapsychology and the later work on the drives, then looping back to his early preoccupations with the wish for love dispersed into knowledge, morality, and loss. We took this approach in the last chapter on group psychology. By now, readers may see why there is no direct line to Freud, psychoanalysis, or education. This recursive style is one way to pressure the question of psychological significance with his metapsychology of learning and to consider the vulnerabilities of education's own wishes for completion.

We will present the problem of representing the psychical apparatus through an original dilemma in education. It has to do with the uneven, conflictive relation between meaning and experience that can be met by the teacher's willingness to extend the educational fold with ideas that defy ordinary modes of thought. Point eight in this chapter's epigram serves as our warning: both pleasure and reality will be difficult to know. We need to ask how those other theories of learning—developed here as wild education and that inevitably underscore pedagogical efforts—gain their significance from attention to the learner's psychological momentum, libidinality, and transference to the external world of others. The large questions are surprising: how does the human tolerate existence, and what qualifies our educational situation?

A GAIN IN PSYCHOLOGICAL SIGNIFICANCE

For psychoanalysis to be interested in the question of significance, theorizing mechanisms of the mind could not be mechanistic, only psychological: soft, tender, susceptible to the world of others, and vulnerable to their own yearnings, fantasies, drives, and desire. Freud then had to imagine what it is like for the elemental human— given the constitutive fact of its infancy, immaturity, and prolonged dependency—to simultaneously notice, apprehend, and lend meaning to the call of both external and internal reality. What can it mean to feel before one knows and to trade in anxiety and satisfaction? This problem of infusing psychological significance yet to be made into the beginning of life brought him to posit internal and external conflicts he supposed formed the mind: the pleasure principle and the reality principle. Both principles would incur problems with love, hate, and ambivalence and shape the destiny of transmitting his metapsychology of learning.

This brief 1911 paper indicates an optimistic stage in psychoanalytic theory and serves as our starting point for discussing education and psychoanalysis from the vantage of their "unsolved problems." Freud's speculation is with the persistence of the mind's infantile roots—its wild education— and he finds evidence in the wish that is woven from bodily events driven by inchoate forces of primal helplessness, pain, and screaming and satiated from being fed, held, and loved. It is the relief from bodily trauma that quickly moves the infant into attention, hallucination, memory of satisfaction, judgment of good and bad, bodily action, and thinking. However, this trajectory of coming into the world also raises a new theoretical problem: the wish is secondary, a defense against primary trauma. We pick up this breakthrough later in the chapter. For the time being, all we have is the fact of the infant's body as sensations and excitations, agony telegraphing absolute need for the other's love. This compost of neoteny is his ancient material: in the realm of the psychical, he always supposes that our earliest bodily experiences create persistent memory traces for the mind's associative pathways. In Freud's view, fantasy, dreaming, thinking, and suffering are never discrete; all are required to make psychology.

Freud was not so satisfied with this paper, even as it sketched the germination of the mind and the photosynthesis of thinking; its bare outline would be elaborated in his second theory of the id, the ego, and the superego, wherein the mind would be given an overabundance of character, with his speculations on the motility of the drives where trauma returns, with the way he grappled with the reality principle in his mass psychological studies, and with his use of myth and literature as exemplary models for affect. External reality, or the world before the subject, would have to pass back through a psychology of love and its loss. In the late Freud, reality and pleasure become more complicated, as does the problem of education. The psychical apparatus, however, continues to be thought of as a system of pressures, tensions, drives, and functions at odds with conscious meanings, motivating the wish, and as proposing estrangement.

Whereas in this early work wishes emerge from the pleasure principle, compel its sexual researches, and catch the subject's subjunctive mood, his late work places new objections, objects, and obstacles into psychical design in the form of pressures or the life and death drives. His great statement on these difficult affairs that include why psychological significance is so easily lost comes with his 1920 study, "Beyond the pleasure principle," and then again in 1930 with his pessimistic survey of culture, "Civilization and its discontents." We return to these two studies shortly. For now, we can say that throughout this work and the transformations he gave to his theories, Freud maintained the ethic of thinking as the means to hold in the mind incompatible ideas and postpone impulsive bodily action, made from a mix-up of the need for security, self-preservation, immediate satisfaction and the demand for love.

As for the problem of psychological significance first raised in 1911, the more Freud's theory progresses into its own obstacles, the more difficult it becomes to decide what is really most traumatic for the impressionable subject: pleasure or reality. This is the key unsolved problem Freud carries over to education and to what we will call his metapsychology of learning. The only advice he gives to educators is the same given to parents and analysts: tell the truth about the world and help move the human beyond wishful thinking. He also knows the difficulty this advice brings because the truth of the world returns everyone to harsh reality and, in actuality, there is really no preparation for existence.

Let us note what Freud means by "thinking." A thinking thought emerges from bodily need for the other and lends veracity to its emotional nature. In essence, thinking is our most personal narrative revolt, as the object of thought is the subject. Initially emerging from the ego's dedication to a refinding in the mind earlier objects of satisfaction experienced in the world, Freud presents thinking as an emotional achievement, a libidinal tie, and a relational event. It is also subject to obsessionality and paranoia and to the ego's mechanisms of defense such as disavowal, or a turning away from reality. A thought presupposes absence and disappearance, and to think is to imagine, symbolize, and read into the difference between the reality principle and the pleasure principle. This means there is something incompatible, and thinking is the mind's capacity to bear mental pain. Only later, after the human has entered language, can thinking be tied to its pleasures of imagination and, to some extent, serve as consolation for what cannot be changed. Thinking, he wrote in this 1911 paper, "is essentially an experimental kind of acting" (p. 221); not pretence for thought but a need for thought to secure the self to enter into the insecurities of the world.

From the side of reason, it makes sense for the notion of education to appear in his 1911 paper; after all, one of the ongoing purposes of school is to learn how to think from the indirections of incompatible experience and encounter the abstract world of knowledge. That is, any education provides experiences for the changing mind. To consider what this work feels like, however, brings education into its own psychology as it, too, is subject to the reality and pleasure principles. The educator's presentation may be overly harsh or so mild that it is missed. As for pedagogy, transmission and reception are typically at odds. The reality of education as well presents a threat or danger to both principles of the mind, as acquiring knowledge means exchanging the known for the unknown, and learning brings incompatible ideas. With all of this come the ego's defenses such as repression, resistance, intellectualization, and denial. Moreover, the teacher is an emotional figure; she or he stands in for the parental and cultural authority, serves as ego ideal and superego, and stirs Oedipal conflicts and the identifications of group psychology. Teachers cannot avoid this emotional world, or psychical reality, and their pedagogical wager is stark: blindness or knowledge, drives or sublimation, insignificance or significance, illusion or mourning.

It is the psychological side of education, where the conflicts between reality and pleasure affect learning, that brings us to our Freudian paradox: because love is already in the learning picture, anxiety over its loss blurs vision. Further, as soon as the unconscious is admitted into this scenery, the very idea of loss, absence, and time, all needed for symbolization, dissolves. The pleasure principle, Freud tells us, equates thought with actuality, refuses difference between the subject and the object, and disregards reality. The unconscious is attraction. Its qualities, pressures, aims, and objects, associated with gratification at all costs, inevitably exchange the problem of judgment for the interdictions of its own authority. As the pleasure principle is a theater of the mind, it cannot be given up.

In Freud's view, and he notes this in his 1911 article, mainly artists find their way into and out of this mess; with imagination, they work within the pleasure principle to create a new reality representing psychological significance. This transforms reality into a problem of narration and interpretation. A few years before he wrote the paper on mental functioning, Freud emphasized this point in a short article, "Creative writers and day-dreaming":

> Might we not say that every child at play behaves like a creative writer, in that he creates a world of his own, or rather, re-arranges the things of his world in a new way which pleases him? It would be wrong to think he does not take the world seriously; on the contrary, he takes his play very seriously and he expends large amounts of emotion on it. The opposite of play is not what is serious but what is real.
>
> (1908, pp. 143–144)

Imagination, or the play of fantasy with representation, is the artist's pleasure principle and royal road to sublimation. And it is for us all.

Yet, what ties education to a psychology of love are myriad human sufferings. So, education cannot proceed without anxiety, and this emotional fact presses on our first education, creating an archive of symptomology and dissolving its terms into unconscious ideation, repression, the compulsion to repeat, and the return of the repressed. Wild education begins life; it refers to introjections, projections, and identifications with family dynamics and group psychology, animates the subject's desire for transference, and carries residues of the affect, anxiety. The unsolved problem is that there can be no education without anxiety; yet, too much anxiety overwhelms the subject who takes cover in defense, inhibitions, and delusion. Too little anxiety underwhelms and leaves the subject isolated.

We see glimpses of this love dilemma in our opening quotation. There Freud (1911) posits that the educator must lean on an offer of love but, in so doing, takes the side of the pleasure principle. This principle emerges from the equation of love with immediate satisfaction and release from internal frustration. Anything frustrating is equated with badness, and so the pleasure principle avoids whatever gets in its way. Yet because we are speaking of learning and encountering the unknown or the demand to think, there is no escape from frustration: it is a situation that also qualifies trying to learn but can be and usually is first felt as a loss of love, and its punishment is bad feelings. Now this simple speculation concerns the unconscious psychical life and emerges from the psychoanalytic idea that to analyze anxieties in learning, the educator must also see herself or himself as having the role of a frustrating object, delaying immediate gratification and proposing learning's abstractions, difficulties, and delay. In this sense, educators call upon the reality principle and risk their own wish to be loved in the process.

In the emotional situation of teaching and learning, there is no immunity for the educator whose own authority is carried away by her or his subjunctive mood made from infantile wishes, libido, anxiety, and guilt. That education is always an emotional situation is not so much the problem, but how to create psychological significance is. That the emotional world is considered insignificant, however, is cruel repression. Yet, it also appears as if Freud is always indexing two conflicted poles of education: the pleasure principle—subjected to the primary processes of the archaic, the unconscious, and the infantile and that serve as the material for the imagination, dreams, and creative life—*and* the reality principle, subjected to the secondary processes of the conscious, the symbolic, and the historical and so serving as the material for the pain of absence, separation, and loss. Later, as the psychical apparatus becomes more like an internal world of object relations (id, ego, superego), superego anxiety and guilt bring Freud to think of education as tied to the problem of happiness, guilt and the need to be punished, and aggression. Why, over his many versions of education, do love and anxiety over its loss serve as the learning linchpin and weak spot?

GAMES

To understand the Freudian paradox of education—that education recapitulates individual development and cultural frustration and its actions break apart development's logic— we are asked to think of learning through the conflicts of its metapsychology and conceive estrangement in education as an after-effect of the ego's love predicament with other egos, with knowledge, with reality, and with itself.

At this point, we can notice three dimensions of education vying for attention: education as a human institution made from libidinal relations between teachers and students and so as group psychology; education as composed from the conflict between the pleasure principle and the reality principle and so as subject to thinking; and wild education as consequent to psychical representatives and the drive to know and so as unconscious. Their contiguity composes the valence and involution of emotional life; all lean on the promise of love.

Perhaps the most poignant example Freud gives to this third sense of education—its wildly creative side —is found in "Beyond the pleasure principle." It comes in the form of his comments on a child's game. In an odd way, it was a child's game with a toy that reshuffled the elements of his previous theories and, in doing so, returned the problem of psychological significance, now from the vantage of symbolizing absence and reappearance.

Here Freud returns to grand speculations on the psychical apparatus with an attempt to consider biology as psychology. The gamble is that the indeterminacy of biological life proposes problems of representation and significance or, in other words, the question *why?* The psychology he has in mind is the compulsion to repeat, and this compulsion goes beyond pleasure and breaks open his first rule that pleasure is the primary motivation animating psychical life. With his study, the pleasure principle is at best only a tendency and is no longer opposed by the reality principle that seeks the delay of satisfaction. Something within pleasure opposes itself and yet, the pleasure principle seems to be the only representative for sexuality:

> The pleasure principle long persists, however, as the method of working employed by the sexual instincts, which are so hard to "educate," and, starting from those instincts, or in the ego itself, it often succeeds in overcoming the reality principle, to the detriment of the organism as a whole.
>
> (1920a, p. 10)

With mention of the ego, the reality principle is reintroduced and bestowed with its psychology that includes a problem with knowing knowledge. Freud then considers another source of dismay: "*perceptual* unpleasure. It may be perception of pressure by unsatisfied instincts; or it may be external perception which is either distressing in itself or which excites unpleasurable expectations in the mental apparatus—that is, which is recognized by it as a 'danger' (p. 11). Anxiety invigorates the picture.

As for the question of the starring role of anxiety in the creation of psychological significance, Freud found a tentative theory in a game his grandson Ernst played, called by the child "'o-o-o-o' and 'da' game" (pp. 14–15), translated by Freud and his daughter, Sophie, the child's mother, as: *fort* (gone) and *da* (there).

> The child had a wooden reel with a piece of string tied round it. It never occurred to him to pull it along with floor behind him, for instance, and play at its being a carriage. What he did was to hold the reel by the string and very skillfully threw it over the edge of his curtained cot, so that it disappeared into it, and at the same time uttering his expressive "o-o-o-o." He then pulled the reel out of the cot again by the string and hailed its reappearance with a joyful "*da*" [there]. This, then, was the complete game—disappearance and return.
>
> (1920a, p. 15)

The child played this game during the mother's absence, something that must have been felt as disagreeable. His continual playing of this game, however, gave Freud the new question, "How then does his repetition of this distressing experience as a game fit in with the pleasure principle?" (p. 15).

Freud interpreted the child's repetition of the game as a piece of psychology and so as a way to change positions from the one being left to the one who sends the object away. Throwing something away may have been the child's revenge, as if he sent his mother away rather than she leaving him behind. Did the child repeat the game to master separation anxiety, or did the repetition itself lead to a certain pleasure of mastery over anxiety? The question is left open, and Freud ruminates on children's play that, after all, does repeat their interpretations of the adult world, from the side of doing to others what they fear will be done to them. Freud mentions the children's game of playing doctor that leads sexual research and the symbolic equation of illness with punishment. If we think about the torturous game of "playing teacher," it is hardly news to observe the cruelty and sadistic pleasure involved in pushing around those who have the misfortunate of having to play the role of the student and take punishment in the form of bad grades, being yelled at, and having to sit in the corner and miss recess. It is here that we can observe the unconscious equation of learning with needing to be punished or to be taught a lesson.

Even as these games seem to transform unpleasurable experience into something pleasurable, Freud still cannot dismiss his speculation that there is something beyond the pleasure principle. The compulsion to repeat, however, does not incur pleasure, and this leads him to study trauma as an external and internal breach of the protective shield that consciousness has become. It will lead to his hypothesis of the death drive, a force that unbinds, disregards pleasure, and seeks its own extinction. Development, Freud gathers, is no longer on the side of progress and change but carries resistance: a tendency to repeat earlier traumatic events.

It seems we cannot give up playing these childhood games. Indeed, Freud places what is uncanny about them in the transference:

> Patients repeat all of these unwanted situations and painful emotions in the transference and revive them with the greatest ingenuity. They seek to bring about the interruption of the treatment while it is still incomplete; they contrive once more to feel themselves scorned, to oblige the physician to speak severely to them and treat them coldly; they discover appropriate objects for their jealously; instead of the passionately desired baby of their childhood, they produce a plan or a promise of some grand present—which turns out as a rule to be no less unreal. None of these can have produced pleasure in the past, and it might be supposed that they would cause less unpleasure to-day if they emerged as memories or dreams instead of taking the form of fresh experiences ... but no lesson has been learnt from the old activities having led instead only to unpleasure.
>
> (1920a, p. 21)

Still, this observation is puzzling, and Freud can only conclude, "Enough is left unexplained to justify the hypothesis of a compulsion to repeat—something that seems more primitive, more elementary, more instinctual than the pleasure principle which it over-rides" (p. 23).

EDUCATION'S GRANDEUR

That Freud binds psychical conflict to education's wager with love is more than a passing interest; throughout his writing, unconscious motives take on greater complicity with the mythology of the life-and-death drives. It causes him to link education to life's existential problems of unhappiness, aggression, and morality and to ponder the individual's hostility to culture along with culture's hostility to individuals. However, cultural organization cannot force thoughtfulness or perpetual peace or establish a world without violence. Then, specifically in his speculation, "The Future of an Illusion," he doubts whether the human can do away with forms of coercion or education:

> It may be asked where the number of superior, unswerving and disinterested leaders are to come from who are to act as educators of future generations ... The grandeur of the plan and its importance for the future of human civilization cannot be disputed. It is securely based on the psychological discovery that man is equipped with the most varied instinctual dispositions, whose ultimate course is determined by the experiences of early childhood. But for the same reason the limitations of man's capacity for education set bounds to the effectiveness of such a transformation in his culture.
>
> (1927a, pp. 8–9)

All told, education is subject to psychology: the drives, the unconscious, and neurosis. If education must essentially address the ego, Freud implies, it is worth the mental struggle to imagine both the ego's sense of coherence and how the ego falls apart. In his paper "The Ego and Id," the problem is this: "… we see this same ego as a poor creature owing service to three masters and consequently menaced by three dangers: from the external world, from the libido of the id, and from the severity of the super-ego" (1923a, p. 56). It is here that rewards and punishments become the mind's scenery and lost cause.

The original unsolvable problem still stems from the insolvent subject who represses incompatible ideas without questioning why. Both teachers and students repress incompatible ideas, and Freud argued that teachers are obligated to think about learning's condition as the human condition. To the early Freud, education's first line of attack was sexual repression, an anchor for social and individual neurosis. Yet, he also knew that the sexual drives could not be educated. Ultimately, for psychoanalysis, the Enlightenment project of exchanging bad knowledge for good truth failed; the problem was not with knowledge but the idea of what it can be to tell the truth about internal conflicts and external aggression. Enlightenment could not illuminate the problem of unhappiness. By 1926a, Freud's evolving view of the ego, the id, and the superego would cast the shadow of anxiety over the question of the origin of values themselves. This move is notorious and sustained Freud's objection that our highest values were transformations of infantile sexuality and even our best values can take a hostile turn into moral anxiety and melancholia.

Only when Freud began to question his understanding of pleasure and considered something beyond the pleasure principle would two ideas come to dominate psychoanalysis. First, Freud (1923a) transformed his view of the ego ideal, initially made from identifications with a powerful object, into a self-critical internal agency called the *superego*. This agency would be the ego's judge and bring affect to the origins of morality. Its tendency is to pull the ego into guilt and its need for punishment. *The conscience* would be another Freudian term for anxiety and guilt. Second, the ego itself would now be thought of as partially unconscious, as a projection of its own surface, as a defensive structure, as subject to the drives, and as in perpetual conflict with the urges of the id and the obsessive cruelty of the superego. Further complicating this inherent conflict is the ego's relations to the external world, its "third master." However, these conflicts can be treated as objects, not as facts and, with this approach, Freud created a new learning proposal: the ego can narrate and interpret this life world and create new accounts than the ones on offer.

Such internal and external drama brought Freud to think education as in conflict with its own knowledge limits. Any appeal to reason would still have to be taken through the unconscious, the superego, ego defenses, and the transference-love, a new form of resistance. To understand more deeply the vulnerabilities of the subject in relation to the work of learning, then, would require a view of education as capable of questioning its own reality principle and disillusioning its own pleasure principle. The limit and potential of education can then be understood from the vantage of how it handles the volatility of love and even what it can mean to take the side of the ego if the ego is already split.

From 1912 onward, Freud did not know the world without war, and this world of war meant trying to understand the relations among aggression, violence, disavowal, and death. Gradually, education would become associated with this negativity: not as insight but with sublimation and not as enlightenment but as courage to think about the harshness of life, to mourn its inevitable losses, and to symbolize this narrative of learning. Just as the psychoanalyst would invite the patient to return to childhood scenes hardly remembered but still affecting the melancholia of loss, education as well would be given its associative force and taken through its figuration.

narrated as archeology and mythology to analyze fantasy, anxiety, and defense.

Yet, these theoretical moves that seem to personify and impersonate everything also emerge from the rubble of wild education. Freud teaches that it is difficult to imagine the currency of education without returning to well-trodden fantasies of one's own childhood of education, including the need to believe one's own theories. He insists that we are never so far away from this buried experience, and our tendency to compulsively regress to an earlier state and then project infantile theories into contemporaneous ones affects the idea of education and how we give account of it. This return of the repressed is how the unconscious works: no contradiction, time, or negation. Timeless beginnings and our unconscious conveyance of them are one dilemma. In psychical life, where thought perception is equated with the object, there really doesn't seem to be any difference to be made between what happened to us as children and what we think education is all about. Another dilemma comes when Freud turns to unhappiness or discontentment in culture. Then, the character of education is at stake.

Freud's pessimistic proposal on education is given almost 20 years after his mental principle paper and is contained in a footnote found in "Civilization and its discontents." There, the largest objection to education comes from the educator's own pleasure principle, which now involves the idea that satisfaction is the reduction of tension. This change in focus complicates his earlier views on love found in his 1911 paper. Yet, in both the early and late Freud, education presents an area of conflict. On the one side, learning material is made from problems and obstacles within its work of motivating an individual's capacity for thought and sublimation. To do this, the educator must lean on an offer of love that comes with conditions. On the other side is the educator's mode of transmitting knowledge, ostensibly her or his conflict with the reality and pleasure principles. This work as well is disrupted because it is made from the constraints of institutional life and the estranging and unifying qualities of group psychology, discussed in the previous chapter. The residue of identification is then experienced as conflicts with love, truth, gratification, and delay and as rewards and punishments. Yet, his story of education takes on greater complexity; even when education's contiguity is with the human nature that it also effectuates, he also places its work beyond the drives. Freud left us with a question: if education carries the burden of psychical reality through its own genealogy structured by the regressive histrionics of the pleasure principle and if it is also charged with disrupting its repetition compulsion, how does the reality principle come into being? At this point, we can say that adaptation to reality ruins the reality principle as the principle itself is an experiment in thought and leans on imagination.

HELPLESSNESS VERSUS HAPPINESS

Freud can be read as proposing that archaic education is the excess of the human's vulnerability that involves susceptibility to be influenced by what is unknown and so is constituted by primary helplessness. He made this claim early in his 1895 "Project for a Scientific Psychology," wherein he first speculated on our earliest response: screaming. Though "The Project" was his first attempt to sketch the economy of the psychical apparatus, he also swerves into psychological significance: "In this way this path of discharge [screaming] acquires a secondary function of the highest importance, that of *communication*, and the initial helplessness of human beings is the *primal source* of all *moral motives*" (1950, p. 318). This thought returns many years later in his (1930a) study of culture and unhappiness.

What is to be noted is that helplessness transforms meaninglessness with the question of significance. In his

1911 paper, Freud returned to developmental history and considered its urgent beginnings when the neonate feels bodily unpleasure, helplessness, and dependency and, in its own drive to know, cries out for the other. This is the raw material of any learning relationship, a transference wish to refind the lost object of satisfaction with the momentous consequence of fusing inchoate need with desire. The cry—our first objection—announces the neonate's entrance into culture, the world of others, communication, and with this advent of love, the infant's sudden worries over its loss. Absence is the additional element that gives rise to symbolization and thinking. Freud said as much when he watched his grandson at play. To these intimate psychical actions, Freud will overlay culture as learning's estrangement: conflicts within group psychology that begin from introjections of object relations, the family, and the school, all scenes of identifications with affected images (mother, father, siblings, leader, friend, teacher). These compose a metapsychology of learning. In Freud's (1914c) view, they can be understood through the clinical dynamics of remembering, repeating, and working through. The transference-love will lend to any education continuity with mythic time but will also be disrupted by the otherness of new knowledge. Learning holds all of this in store as it repeats and transforms the motives and temporality of psychical economy: helplessness, synthesis, destruction, and creation. In this game of here/gone, the object is brought closer, cast away, and then refound.

We are now ready to ask, given Freud's project and stylistics of transmitting psychoanalysis, what happens to the concept of education and how its account can be given when affected by psychical reality. Freud raised a comparable question in an optimistic early paper carrying the title, "Claims of psychoanalysis to scientific interest." His quick answer would be that the educator suffers from memory problems. In a short section on education, he speculated on what psychoanalysis can contribute to an understanding of educational relations from the vantage of the educator's work:

> Only someone who can feel his way into the minds of children can be capable of educating them; and we grown-up people cannot understand children because we no longer understand our own childhood. Our infantile amnesia proves that we have grown estranged from our childhood.
>
> (1913b, p. 189)

However, something Freud thought almost 10 years later also interferes and is taken into the workings of memory.

Consciousness, Freud tells us in "A note upon the mystic writing pad," arises instead of memory traces. Like the child's writing toy, consciousness is "a receptive surface" (1925c, p. 230) capable of receiving impressions *and* a protective barrier as it is tied to perception, which is a defense against overwhelming external stimuli and involves the wish to erase and begin anew. Writing on the mystic pad, however, does leave a trace in its wax backing. With a child's toy, Freud found a way to explain unconscious effects of growing up and why memory is more than conscious memory.

> If we imagine one hand writing upon the surface of the Mystic Writing-Pad while another periodically raises its covering-sheet from the wax slab, we shall have a concrete representation of the way in which I tried to picture the functioning of the perceptual apparatus of our mind.
>
> (p. 232)

Counter-intuitively, memory is not so much the other side of forgetting as its record. This was one of his old ideas, made from his 1899 speculation on "screen memories," wherein he argued that representations in memory can also be thought through the fragmenting procedures of dream-work: condensation substitution, the reversal of opposites, and displacement. There he also wrote there were no memories in childhood, only memories of childhood.

One's own childhood education is difficult to remember for so many reasons and, to return Freud's observation in "Claims of psychoanalysis to scientific interest," there must be an estrangement between teachers and students. Understanding this estrangement, he felt, could lead educators into an analysis of their own repressions, necessary to understand to question the ways in which education can be in the service of forgetting. At the time of these remarks on the educator's estrangement from the student, Freud felt that significant forgetting had to do with the repression of sexuality. It is not so much that we forget the childhood sexual researches as much as we forget what it feels like to want thrilling, impossible knowledge and persist in making unassailable theories. Educators forget their own urge to know at all costs. They also forget the feeling that, at least for a little while with infantile theories, helplessness and happiness do meet. With the mystic writing pad, however, Freud will find something else forgotten: perception cannot do away with illegibility.

TWO PRINCIPLES OF KNOWLEDGE

When Freud (1911) posits the workings of the psychical apparatus as emerging from the conflicts between the pleasure principle (loosely defined as the immediacy for satisfaction) and the reality principle (loosely thought of as the capacity to delay the pleasure principle by way of the experiments of thought), the psychological origin of the mind is uncertain. So, too, are the definitions of the mind's principles, and he admits that further research into pleasure is necessary. Fantasy, art, sexuality, creative writing, religion, and the unconscious will instruct Freud. As for education, it becomes a frontier concept, situated between these two tendencies because its reality principle is entangled in love, and pedagogical efforts founder upon love's impressions. Only art and its capacity for sublimation, an investment in representations of narrative revolts, can reconcile, or make conscious, these transference effects.

The two formulations of the pleasure and reality principles, sketchy as they are, represent the psyche's objections, objects, and obstacles to learning. However, they may also be considered as principles of knowledge creating our relations to life and death, to imagination and duty, and to our relations with and responsibilities to the world on offer. If the pleasure principle belongs to narcissism, the reality principle will be constituted through loss of the object. In this sense, the reality principle, as Freud (1917c) wrote in his metapsychological paper "Mourning and Melancholia," is associated with and orients the object's loss *and* the ego's struggle to carry out the work of mourning. Learning to live with letting the object go and mourning loss is how Freud thought we become both subject to history and take our place as historical subjects. That humans are transient creatures is the reality principle.

Freud's sketch of mental principles also refers to the unconscious motives that carry dissonance and emotional force within any representation. The pleasure and reality principles situate thought perception as belonging to and expressing the designs of human nature and as beholden to its own beliefs, to believing its beliefs, *and* then to an interest in doubting, with questions, its own nature. This capacity for doubt is where Freud ties education to the question of disillusioning belief in timeless knowledge, immediate satisfaction, and omnipotent thought. These are the contentions the reality principle brings. Essentially, if education comes as a blow to narcissism, it must also propose love's dispersal into new objects with the work of making psychological significance.

The reality principle is never complete, nor can it be, as reality is that which exists without the subject and requires the subject's apprehension, interpretations, and capacity for doubt. This notion of reality is associated with the emergence of waking consciousness and its awareness of the external world of others. The principle itself focuses the ego with its relationships to its objects and brings to the fore incompatible ideas. Freud felt his paper as "preparatory rather than expository"; it closes with an address to the reader:

> In these few remarks on the psychical consequences of adaptation to the reality principle I have been obliged to adumbrate views which I should have preferred for the present to withhold and whose justification will certainly require no small effort. But I hope it will not escape the notice of the benevolent reader how in these pages too the dominance of the reality principle is beginning.
>
> (1911, p. 226)

It must have taken a great deal of courage to bring into representation glimmers of ideas incompatible to consciousness, and Freud's (1911) paper is difficult to characterize. It reads like a phenomenology of ontology in that with each and every perception the human takes into itself, consciousness presents as affecting its own design and as creating associative pathways: memory links among satisfaction, objects, affects, words, and ideas. The elements of consciousness and its emergence are imagined through transformations of internal need and bodily action. As much as these procedures characterize the propulsive birth of the historical subject and its tenacity with the pleasure principle, these movements of thought open emotional life. They also serve as an index to the sudden and traumatic awareness of being in the world of others met with the wish to take this world into the mind and to refind there lost objects in the world. What is lost concerns that which is absent or missing, and thinking thoughts are our greatest substitute, a work of the mind that preserves the object in memory, narrates passing time, and constructs history. Thinking permits affects their ideas.

The psychological nature of apprehending reality and pleasure through interpreting their force is another way into the question of how psychological significance is made from libidinal attachments. With psychology, reality and pleasure are two sides of the same coin. Freud asks whether reality can be thought of as a personal acquisition, a thing in itself, or a judgment of the ego confronting its own fantastical limits. So, reality is posited in two of its psychological dimensions: dream life compresses psychical reality, and with the external world comes the possibility of constructing historical reality. Both gravitate to the wish, influenced as they are by the desire for love, recognition, and memory. Both index their history of loss and autobiography of attachments.

Freud's incidental notes on education, juxtaposed with his point on the unconscious, can be read as proposing the problem of psychological significance because to approach the idea of a psychical apparatus in relation to the outside world always raises the question of why learning occurs, how it proceeds, what stops it short, and why judgments take a detour through desire, pleasure, and wish. If education must trade in love and authority, it, too, like the family and group psychology, becomes a laboratory for transference of human nature, and its experiments with reality pressure the subject's affect with thinking. Freud's lifelong studies of the proclivities of neurosis as a means to understand any human conflict gave him some clues as to the force of reality:

> Neurotics turn away from reality because they find it unbearable—either the whole or parts of it. ... And we are now confronted with the task of investigating the development of the relation of neurotics and of mankind in general to reality, and in this way of bringing the

psychological significance of the real external world into the structure of our theories.

(1911, p. 218)

Add to this his view that sexual drives cannot be educated and we can begin to consider what is in store for the very thought of education and perhaps why psychoanalysis presents education as a conflictive emotional situation and as an unsolved problem that requires a narrative unafraid of unsettling itself.

In fact, we can surmise that Freud is saying that to understand education—what it is like to need education, to encounter knowledge, to make an idea, to take the self as an object of learning, to anticipate learning and its failure—relies on the passionate embrace of the pleasure principle. Again, Freud reminds his readers that psychoanalysis begins with an interest in the unconscious, itself ruled by the pleasure principle or primary thought processes of timelessness, no negation, and the rule of contiguity, or equation of contradictory thoughts and things. The struggle with reality, frustration, and the outside world, however, provides a portal into the problem of incompatible thoughts: that satisfaction in the mind is at odds with both actions in the world and the demands of others. The paradox is that imagination emerges from the struggle between the reality and pleasure principles. It is also our most serious play.

If at first Freud presents the ego as a consequence of its calculations and as trading fantasy for reality, he also proposes that the ego is a precipice of lost objects, identifications, and its history of love. So, a clear distinction between reality and pleasure is the ego's fragile spot. This burdens educators with the view that for the pedagogical relation to be capable of and interested in the reality principle, they must also lean upon offers of love. In so doing, educators are then subject to their own development and the repetition of their own history of refinding lost objects, in learning for love, and in their own slow transformation of infantile theories of learning.

Freud's work on the life and death drives brought new depth to the ego and complicated the reality and pleasure principles. In analyzing the ego's tendency toward feelings of inferiority, Freud speculated that repressed infantile sexuality must be accompanied by painful feelings:

> Loss of love and failure leave behind them a permanent injury to self regard in the form of a narcissistic scar ... The child's sexual researches, on which limits are imposed by his physical development, lead to no satisfactory conclusion; hence such later complaints as "I can't accomplish anything; I can't succeed in anything." The lessening amount of affection he receives, the increasing demands of education, hard words and an occasional punishment—these show him at last the full extent to which he has been scorned.
>
> (1920a, pp. 20, 21)

A compulsion to repeat these early developments is the first material of any learning that both animates our "narcissistic scar" and its negation.

In subjecting education to the problem of the reality and pleasure principles, we can begin to see that education is always a relationship constituted and threatened by intersubjectivity. This allows Freud to transfer to education a clinical and existential protest: what can access to reality mean if reality is always interpreted reality and so a problem of perception, judgment, and love? His early article of 1911 introduces the vague notion of the ego's work of reality testing. He means to distinguish how the ego differentiates between perception from hallucination and then the inner world and the external one.

Yet, not until his paper "Negation" would Freud challenge the psychoanalyst to take seriously the conflict between words and things and to listen differently to the protest over the difference between what is said and what one cannot yet say. The opening of this paper also gives some technical advice:

> The manner in which our patients bring forward their associations during the work of analysis gives us an opportunity for making some interesting observations. "Now you'll think I mean to say something insulting, but really I've no such intention." We realize that this is a rejection, by projection, of an idea that has just come up. Or: "You ask who this person in the dream can be. It's *not* my mother." We emend this to: "So it *is* his mother." In our interpretation, we take the liberty of disregarding the negation and of picking out the subject-matter alone of the association.
>
> (1925b, p. 235)

Again, we see Freud grappling with the problem of psychological significance, now from the vantage of a split between intellectual resistance and emotional acceptance. The early problem of reality testing is reformulated: its work is

> not to find an object in real perception which corresponds to the one presented, but to refind such an object, to convince oneself that it is still there ... But it is evident that a precondition for the setting up of reality-testing is that objects shall have been lost which once brought real satisfaction.
>
> (1925b, 237–238)

The reality principle is our best doubt; it tests the relation between disappearance and return.

Memory registers and inherits this dilemma, posting technical conflicts in the clinic and epistemological confusion as to the reach of truth and reality. Freud hints at the difficulty of this alliance in the earlier paper on mental functioning with his eighth point:

> But one must never allow oneself to be misled into applying the
> standards of reality to repressed psychical structures, and on that
> account, perhaps, into undervaluing the importance of phantasies
> in the formation of symptoms on the ground that they are not
> actualities, or into tracing a neurotic sense of guilt back to some other
> sources because there is no evidence that any actual crime has been
> committed.

> (1911, p. 225)

UNHAPPINESS AND AGGRESSION

"Civilization and Its Discontents" revises the struggle between
the reality and pleasure principle. Both are taken through the
ravages of human aggression, or "what men themselves show
by their behaviour to be the purpose of life" (1930a, p. 76).
If we speak of "oceanic feelings" (1930a, p. 64), Freud finds
beneath the rhapsody of unity an infantile world, a desire for
an unencumbered pleasure principle, a free reign of drives, and
a wish for a world without obstacles. Yet, in Freud's vocabulary,
this archaic principle limits its own unfolding as pleasure refers
to the need to release rising tension. This is what Freud means
by the relief of satisfaction. However, what the individual wants,
Freud finds, is restricted by their constitution. He tells us that it
is easier to experience unhappiness: "An unrestricted satisfaction
of every need presents itself as the most enticing method of
conducting one's life, but it means putting enjoyment before
caution, and soon brings its own punishment" (1930a, p. 77).

There is no protection against suffering, and love will open its
gates: "It is that we are never so defenseless against suffering as
when we love, never so helplessly unhappy as when we have lost
our loved object or its love" (1930a, p. 82). Freud concludes: "The
programme of becoming happy, which the pleasure principle
imposes on us cannot be fulfilled; yet we must not—indeed,
we cannot—give up our efforts to bring it nearer to fulfillment
by some other means" (p. 83). Whatever means are available,

whatever the external world has on offer, Freud sees psychical reality as mediating fulfillment and as creating an unknown factor: more conflict. With this insistence, he parts ways from theories of socialism, religion, programs of betterment, and social eugenics. Suffering cannot be eliminated as, for Freud, it is both the human condition and that which allows conditions to be human.

Freud's understanding of civilization emerges from this discussion on suffering, and his etymology can be read as indexing conflicts in education.

> The word civilization (*Kultur*) describes the whole sum of the achievements and the regulations which distinguish our lives from those of our animal ancestors and which serve two purposes—namely to protect men against nature and to adjust their mutual relations.
>
> (1930a, p. 88)

Yet culture provokes what Freud calls "cultural frustration" (p. 97) made from a combustible mix of individual desire, its own constitutional limits, and the demands of the social upon individual development. If Freud is grappling with the great question of where our misery comes from, he will also insist that civilization will not be so much the cause of unhappiness as it will be its container and the means to overcome its own unhappy nature. With its prohibitions and laws, culture will provide a screen for the death drive.

At this point in his study of civilization, Freud turns to myth. We saw this move in the last chapter on group psychology, and it is Freud's means to speculate on why there is culture at all. He takes yet another detour into the thickets of prehistory by imagining prehistoric man's progression from haphazard nature to signification. He speculates that sexuality itself is consequential:

> One may suppose that the founding of families was connected with the fact that a moment came when the need for genital satisfaction no longer made its appearance like a guest who drops in suddenly, and, after his departure, is heard of no more for a long time, but instead took up its quarters as a permanent lodger.
>
> (1930a, p. 99)

When love trumps necessity and when sexuality can be represented, the human enters cultural life, a mythology of origins, and the world of emotions, all of which index libidinal ties. With the advent of culture, sexuality can now be unhinged from nature and its necessities, and limits on sexuality become culture's unsolved problems. Yet, the large problem of Freud's study concerns human aggression, and "In consequence to this mutual hostility of human beings, civilized society is perpetually threatened with disintegration" (1930a, p. 112). This is culture's unsolved problem.

By the end of his study, Freud is well aware that he is analyzing culture as if it mirrored individual life and so knows that he is extending his theories with poetic license:

> There is one question which I can hardly evade. If the development of civilization has such a far-reaching similarity to the development of the individual and if it employs the same methods, may we not be justified in reaching the diagnosis, that under the influence of cultural urges, some civilizations, or some epochs of civilization—possibly the whole of mankind—have become 'neurotic'?
>
> (1930a, p. 144)

Even institutions are accorded their psychical life and neurotic trends. He also wonders what use such a diagnosis can have. It is almost as if he is on the verge of asking his 1911 question: how can the knowledge of psychoanalysis become psychologically significant?

Freud does provide a way into why there is a need to understand social neurosis and its turn away from reality when he takes a survey of formal education. In a footnote, he names the two concealments in the curriculum of schools: alongside its eschewal of sexuality,

> Its other sin is that it does not prepare [young people] for the aggressiveness of which they are destined to become the objects. In sending the young out into life with such a false psychological orientation, education is behaving as though one were to equip people starting on a Polar expedition with summer clothing and maps of the Italian Lakes. In this it becomes evident that a certain misuse is being made of ethical demands.
>
> (1930a, p. 134)

EDUCATION: *SEE UNDER UNSOLVED PROBLEMS OF*

The index of the *Standard Edition* of Freud's work contains a midsize entry on education and concludes with a reference to its unsolved problems. The greatest unsolved problem is love. This detail becomes for our study a provocation for wide-ranging associations and resistance to their lines of flight. To imagine education as both an unsolved problem and as a nexus of its creation gives us pause. More often than not, there is little toleration for problems that cannot be solved, and the wish for education for whatever age is, after all, on the side of actions, deliberations, and rescue. The promise of its knowledge is that skills, once learned and applied, will solve problems, not cause more of them. Yet, the tendency to reduce education to its socialization function and to a child's being educated carries its own dysfunctions. We miss the workings of love and its potential as the means to symbolize our uncertainties and reach into what is sublime in any learning: the existential experience of learning from conflicts, the slow work of tolerating incompatible ideas, the chance to move beyond the directions of experience, the fragile interest in symbolizing reality, and the courage of narrative revolts. These elements are needed if education is to be affected by the ongoing problem of psychological significance and if the question of love is to be given its due and purposes.

In the Freudian vocabulary, the concept of education becomes an exercise in free association and narrative revolts. It refers to its everyday occurrences: that is, to upbringing, schools, and the teacher's conflicts. Then come the affected processes involved—helplessness, influence, and susceptibility—met by culture's demands. Education's own principles of knowledge waver between the poles of pleasure and reality. Optimistically, education is also linked to the prevention of war, to sexual enlightenment, and to the checking of infantile sexuality. Interminably, it is related to and affected by the workings of the psyche and its potential for imagination and sublimation. There are unconscious registrations and, at times, education is like the mystic writing pad. From the negative side, education is associated with the development of a sense of guilt, the superego, anxiety, the Oedipus complex, and group psychology. Its weakest form will take shape in hypnotic suggestion and hallucination. The unsolved problems of education bring Freud into his major concepts of psychoanalysis, objects of knowledge lost and found in the transference, the ego, love, authority, and disavowal. *Education* may be another term that signifies the problem of learning, configures the contentious history of transmitting psychoanalysis, and gestures toward the human condition of learning for love and forgetting its lessons. Education in the Freudian archive is always tied to the practitioners' unconscious resistance, to the fact of their natality, and to their psychical life. The need for education also affects what becomes of it. The work of education will always be interminable because it is always incomplete and because it animates our incompleteness.

With the need for education comes the need for teachers. Only once did Freud address them directly. In his preface to August Aichhorn's psychoanalytic study on youth, Freud's concludes with encouragement in the form of an invitation:

> I will end with a further inference, and this time one which is important not for the theory of education but for the status of those who are engaged in education. If one has learnt analysis by experiencing it on his own person and is in a position of being able to employ it in borderline and mixed cases to assist him in his work, he should obviously be given the right to practice analysis, and narrow-minded motives should not be allowed to try to put obstacles in his way.
>
> (1925d, pp. 274–275)

In this rejoinder, Freud also requests that we sweep away objections in our path for a view of something better and more uncertain: freedom of thought and open minds.

READING PROBLEMS

In placing education into the field of unsolved problems, readers may now wonder what to do. However, there is no getting rid of love, so Freud's psychoanalysis begins with a prior question: what has already happened? An analytic approach, he supposed, might open new learning dispositions by taking apart the old uncanny ones. With these narrative revolts, Freud teaches that the work of construction is doing something to our knowledge: experimenting with its limits, taking on incompatible ideas, and gambling with a gain in meaning. This may be one of the reasons why he turned so often to literature, myth, and the poet's license. There, affects are given free play in symbolization. Literature returns our objections as representations and turns incompatible ideas into constructions of affected knowledge. Readers must look into meaning, imagine things that are absent, and take their reading practices as an object, objection, and obstacle to thought. On this view, literature challenges readers to become wild psychoanalysts. We follow Freud's lead and return to one of his friends, the writer Thomas Mann, to conclude our study with open-end literary affairs.

Thomas Mann's psychoanalytic novel, *Magic Mountain*, holds clues to our pedagogical illness. Much of his novel plays out between the figures of two teachers fighting to influence their pupil Hans Castrop. Both were caught between the poles of the pleasure and reality principles, yet neither managed to understand the psychological significance of their theories, nor did they care from whence their theories came. Instead, each was taken over by their love cause. Settembrini's cause was human progress through the promise of reason. He was one of Hans Castrop's two teachers. His pedagogy involved explaining the world of pain. Settembrini was also a patient in the sanitarium where the novel unfolds. At their first encounter, as Settembrini explains to Hans his unending research project, under the encyclopedic title *The Sociology of Suffering*, he is also compelled to answer his own questions. We break into the middle of his speech:

> In which human sufferings of all classes and species will be treated in detailed, exhaustive, systematic faction. You will object: What good are classes, species, and systems? And I reply: Order and classification are the beginning of mastery, whereas the truly dreadful enemy is the unknown. The human race must be led out of the primitive stage of fear and long-suffering vacuity and into a phase of purposeful activity … only when one first recognizes their causes and negates them, and that almost all sufferings of the individual are illnesses of the social organism.

(2005, pp. 292–293)

Settembrini imagines he knows the cause of misery but cannot see misery in his own lost cause.

The other teacher is Herr Naphta, Settembrini's nemesis. His pedagogy insisted on the violent underside of Enlightenment. The human, this pedagogue yelled, cannot transcend desire, and desire is subject to our nervous condition. Reason, health, and virtue meant nothing to him. As he insisted that nothing would unify the human, he could not notice how he was falling apart. All told, Herr Naphta's pedagogy taught that illness was the human condition

> because to be human was to be ill. Indeed, man was ill by nature, his illness was what made him human, and whoever sought to make him healthy and attempted to get him to make peace with nature, to "return to nature" (whereas he had never been natural), that whole pack of Rousseauian prophets—regenerators, vegetarians, fresh-air freaks, sunbath apostles, and so forth—wanted nothing more than to dehumanize man and turn him into an animal ...
>
> (2005, pp. 550–551)

Now the conflict between these two versions of pedagogy— between Rousseau and Nietzsche—takes up a great deal of this novel. Today, we might consider this as the fight between humanism and poststructuralism wherein both claim the problem of the human but to different ends. Eventually, the war of objections between these teachers forgot the complications of wild education. Their argument ended badly. They could imagine only settling it with a duel. That, too, brought no satisfaction. Settembrini is still not sure he is taken seriously, so he shoots his gun into the air, leaving the next move to Naphta, who shoots himself in the head.

As for Hans Castorp, who witnessed this mess of constructions and became influenced by one teacher and then the other, until they were almost cancelled out, he soon had to leave the Magic Mountain, only to become lost on a battlefield in the First World War. Mann stays with this terrible problem of war's meaninglessness, as did Freud.

Let us make a note on pedagogy, trace its roots to our wild education, and read Mann's fantasy of two teachers as if they were a combined figure, a psychical representative of the two sides of the pedagogical coin. When pedagogy can only be tossed into the air, the game is split into winners and losers. Mann, however, gives us a survey of this arbitrary gamble. So we might also read Mann's novel as his literary intervention, a representation of this "fort da" game we play. Our wager is that pedagogy does not have to end this way; if it must be lost, it can also be refound.

The schoolroom of the mind presents the unconscious dimensions of education's registrations, an index of love's impressions and a prehistory of learning for love that also composes wild education. In this otherworld, magical thinking, fantasy, omnipotence, and the infantile coexist along with the ego's anxieties of losing love. In the logic of the unconscious, learning and Eros equate and find their second life in the transference, another term for learning. Yet, there is no originary moment for the representation of learning. Indeed, learning gambles with the raw material of love's history, an incitement to education. The best Freud's psychoanalysis could do was to urge the narrative right of free association and then listen to all things utterly human: screaming, helplessness, and potential. These are the raw material for narrative revolts and the royal road to its uncertainties.

Representing this mutability and interpreting learning as transformation brings social, cultural, and emotional constraints into an analysis of their symbolization. We may need to mix metaphors. The soft middle ground is where our objections can be taken so seriously that we need not sink. We can make from their impressions objects of knowledge that then revise our approach to our obstacles in narrating learning. We have now reached the difficult psychoanalytic idea of the influencing unconscious and bodily drives that insist without reason, history, and narrative but can be subject to them all. Timeless education, Freud teaches, is our greatest obstacle to and objection in learning. Narrative, or putting these things to words for analysis, is our way to tell time, let it pass, and create anew. Yet, the immaterial and often lost object relations of education—love, resistance, anxiety, and defense—are themselves the push for psychological significance. Education, it turns out, has much ado. Thinking this "wild education" may open new ways to return to Freud and analyze our current education by inviting along the subject who dreams and wishes to wake up.

REFERENCES

Appignanesi, Lisa, and John Forrester. 1992. *Freud's women*. New York: Basic Books.

Bass, Alan. 1998. Sigmund Freud: The question of a Weltanschauung and of defense. In *Psychoanalytic versions of the human condition: Philosophies of life and their impact on practice*, ed. Paul Marcus and Alan Rosenberg, 412–446. New York: New York Universities Press.

Brecht, Karen, Volker Friedrich, Ludger M. Hermanns, Isidor J. Kaminer, and Dierk H. Juelich, eds. 1993. *"Here life goes on in a most peculiar way ...": Psychoanalysis before and after 1933*. English edition prepared by Hella Ehlers. Trans. Christine Trollope. Hamburg: Kellner Verlag.

Breger, Louis. 2000. *Freud: Darkness in the midst of vision*. New York: Wiley and Sons.

Britzman, Deborah P. 1998. *Lost subjects, contested objects: Toward a psychoanalytic inquiry of learning*. Albany: State University of New York Press.

——. 2003a. *After-education: Anna Freud, Melanie Klein and psychoanalytic histories of learning*. Albany: State University of New York Press.

——. 2003b. *Practice makes practice: A critical study of learning to teach*, revised edition. Albany: State University of New York Press.

——. 2007. *Novel education: Psychoanalytic studies of learning and not learning.* New York: Peter Lang Press.

——. 2009. *The very thought of education: Psychoanalysis and the impossible professions.* Albany: State University of New York Press.

Cavell, Marcia. 1993. *The psychoanalytic mind: From Freud to philosophy.* Cambridge, MA: Harvard University Press.

Edmundson, Mark. 2007. *The death of Sigmund Freud: The legacy of his last days.* New York: Bloomsbury USA.

Engelman, Edmund. 1976. *Berggasse 19: Sigmund Freud's home and offices, Vienna 1938: The photographs of Edmund Engelman*, Intro. by Peter Gay. New York: Basic Books.

Felman, Shoshana. 1992. Education and crisis, or the vicissitudes of teaching. In *Testimony: Crisis of witnessing in literature, psychoanalysis, and history*, ed. Shoshana Felman and Dori Laub, 1–56. New York: Routledge.

Freud, Anna. 1981. A study guide to Freud's writing (1978 [1977]). In *Psychoanalytic psychology of normal development 1970–1980, the writings of Anna Freud,* vol. VIII, 209–276. New York: International University Press.

The Freud Museum. 1998. *20 Maresfield Gardens: A guide to the Freud museum.* London: Serpent's Tail.

Freud, Sigmund. 1953–1974. *The standard edition of the complete psychological works of Sigmund Freud.* Ed. and trans. James Strachey, in collaboration with Anna Freud, 24 vols. London: Hogarth Press and Institute for Psychoanalysis.

——, and Joseph Breuer. 1893–95. *Studies on hysteria.* SE 2, 2–319.

——. 1896. Heredity and the aetiology of the neuroses. SE 3, 143–56.

——. 1897a. Letter 71 (October 15, 1897). SE 1, 263–266.

——. 1897b. Letter 73 (October 31, 1897). SE 1, 267.

——. 1899. Screen memories. SE 3, 303–22.

——. 1900a. *The interpretation of dreams (first part).* SE 4, xxiii–338.

——. 1900b. *The interpretation of dreams (second part).* SE 5, 339–627.

——. 1901. *The psychopathology of everyday life.* SE 6, 1–310.

——. 1905a [1901]. Fragment of an analysis of a case of hysteria. SE 7, 7–122.

——. 1905b. *Jokes and their relation to the unconscious.* SE 8, 9–258.

——. 1905c. Three essays on the theory of sexuality. SE 7, 130–245.

——. 1908 [1907]. Creative writers and day-dreaming. SE 9, 143–153.

——. 1909 [1908]. Family romances. SE 9, 237–241.

——. 1910a [1909]. Five lectures on psycho-analysis. SE 11, 9–55.

——. 1910b. A special type of choice of object made by men (contributions to the psychology of love I). SE 11, 165–175.

——. 1910c. "Wild" psycho-analysis. SE 11, 221–227.

——. 1911. Formulations on the two principles of mental functioning. SE 12, 218–226.

——. 1912. The dynamics of transference. SE 12, 97–108.

——. 1913a. On beginning the treatment (further recommendations on the technique of psycho-analysis I). SE 12, 123–144.

——. 1913b. The claims of psycho-analysis to scientific interest. SE 13, 165–190.

——. 1913c [1912–13]. Totem and taboo: Some points of agreement between the mental lives of savages and neurotics. SE 13, xiii–161.

——. 1914a. On the history of the psycho-analytic movement. SE 14, 7–66.

——. 1914b. On narcissism: An introduction. SE 14, 73–102.

——. 1914c. Remembering, repeating and working-through (further recommendations on the technique of psycho-analysis II). SE 12, 145–156.

——. 1914d. Some reflections on a schoolboy psychology. SE 13, 241–244.

——. 1915a. Instincts and their vicissitudes. SE 14, 117–140.

——. 1915b [1914]. Observations on transference-love (further recommendations on the technique of psycho-analysis III). SE 12, 159–171.

——. 1915c. The unconscious. SE 14, 166–215.

——. 1916–1917 [1915–1917]. *Introductory lectures on psycho-analysis (parts I and II)*. SE 15, 9–239.

——. 1917a. A difficulty in the path of psycho-analysis. SE 17, 137–144.

——. 1917b [1916–17]. *Introductory lectures on psycho-analysis (part III)*. SE 16, 243–496.

——. 1917c [1915]. Mourning and melancholia. SE 14, 243–258.

——. 1919a. "A child is being beaten": A contribution to the study of the origin of sexual perversions. SE 17, 179–204.

——. 1919b [1918]. On the teaching of psycho-analysis in universities. SE 17, 169–173.

——. 1919c. The "uncanny." SE 17, 219–256.

——. 1920a. Beyond the pleasure principle. SE 18, 7–64.

——. 1920b. A note on the prehistory of the technique of analysis. SE 18, 263–265.

——. 1921. Group psychology and the analysis of the ego. SE 18, 69–143.

——. 1923a. The ego and the id. SE 19, 12–66.

——. 1923b [1922]. Two encyclopedia articles. SE 18, 235–259.

——. 1925a. An autobiographical study. SE 20, 7–74.

——. 1925b. Negation. SE 19, 235–239.

——. 1925c [1924]. A note upon the "Mystic writing-pad." SE 19, 227–232.

——. 1925d. Preface to Aichhorn's *Wayward youth*. SE 19, 273–275.

——. 1925e. The resistances to psycho-analysis. SE 19, 213–222.

——. 1926a [1925]. Inhibitions, symptoms and anxiety. SE 20, 87–174.

——. 1926b. The question of lay analysis: Conversations with an impartial person. SE 20, 183–250.

——. 1927a. The future of an illusion. SE 21, 5–56.

——. 1927b. Postscript. SE 20, 251–258.

——. 1930a [1929]. Civilization and its discontents. SE 21, 64–157.

——. 1930b. The Goethe prize. SE 21, 208–212.

——. 1932. My contact with Joseph Popper-Lynkeus. SE 22, 219–224.

——. 1933 [1932]. New introductory lectures on psycho-analysis. SE 22, 5–182.

——. 1935. To Thomas Mann on his sixtieth birthday. SE 22, 255.

——. 1937a. Analysis terminable and interminable. SE 23, 216–253.

——. 1937b. Constructions in analysis. SE 23, 257–269.

——. 1939 [1934-38]. Moses and monotheism: Three essays. SE 23, 7–137.

——. 1940a [1938]. An outline of psycho-analysis. SE 23, 144–207.

——. 1940b [1938]. Some elementary lessons in psycho-analysis. SE 23, 281–286.

——. 1940c [1938]. Splitting of the ego in the process of defense. SE 23, 275–278.

——. 1950 [1895]. Project for a scientific psychology. SE 1, 295–343.

Gamwell, Lynn. 1989. The origins of Freud's antiquities collection. In *Sigmund Freud and art: His personal collection of antiquities*, ed. Lynn Gamwell and Richard Wells, 21–32. Binghamton: State University of New York.

Gay, Peter. 1988. *Freud: A life for our time*. New York: W. W. Norton & Company, Inc.

Goggin, James, and Eileen Brockman Goggin. 2001. *Death of a "Jewish science": Psychoanalysis in the Third Reich*. West Lafayette, IN: Purdue University Press.

Greenberg, Valerie D. 1997. *Freud and his aphasia book: Language and the sources of psychoanalysis*. Ithaca: Cornell University Press.

Grubrich-Simitis, Ilse. 1996. *Back to Freud's texts: Making silent documents speak*. Trans. Philip Slokin. New Haven: Yale University Press.

Jones, Ernst. 1972. *Sigmund Freud, life and work: Vol. 1, The young Freud, 1856-1900*. London: Hogarth Press.

——. 1974a. *Sigmund Freud, life and work: Vol. II, Years of maturity, 1901-1919*. London: Hogarth Press.

——. 1974b. *Sigmund Freud, life and work: Vol. III, The last phase, 1919-1939*. London: Hogarth Press.

Kerr, John. 2001. Group psychology and the analysis of the ego (1921): The text. In *On Freud's "Group psychology and the analysis of the ego*," ed. E. S. Person, 3–36. Hillsdale, N.J.: Analytic Press.

Kofman, Sarah. 1985. *The enigma of woman: Woman in Freud's writings.* Trans. Catherine Porter. Ithaca: Cornell University Press.

Kristeva, Julia. 1995. *New maladies of the soul.* Trans. Ross Guberman. New York: Columbia University Press.

———. 2000. *The sense and non-sense of revolt: The powers and limits of psychoanalysis.* Trans. Jeanine Herman. New York: Columbia University Press.

Laplanche, J., and J.-B. Pontalis. 1973. *The language of psychoanalysis.* Trans. Donald Nicholson-Smith. New York: W. W. Norton & Company.

Makari, George. 2008. *Revolution in mind: The creation of psychoanalysis.* New York: HarperCollins Publishers.

Mann, Thomas. 1957. Freud and the future (1936). In *Essays by Thomas Mann,* trans. H. T. Lowe-Porter, 303–324. New York: Vintage Books.

———. 2005 [1924]. *The magic mountain: A novel.* Trans. John E. Woods. Toronto: A. A. Knopf.

May, Ulrike. 2008. Nineteen patients in analysis with Freud (1910–1920). *American Imago* 65(1), 41–105.

Person, Ethel Spector, ed. 2001. *On Freud's "Group psychology and the analysis of the ego."* Hillsdale, NJ: Analytic Press.

Ricoeur, Paul. 1970. *Freud and philosophy: An essay on interpretation.* Trans. Denis Savage. New Haven, CT: Yale University Press.

Rieff, Phillip. 1979. *Freud: The mind of the moralist, third edition.* Chicago: University of Chicago Press.

Sachs, David. 1971. On Freud's doctrine of emotion. In *Freud: A collection of essays,* ed. Richard Wollheim, 132–146. New York: Anchor/Doubleday Press.

Spitz, Ellen Handler. 1994. Promethean positions. In *Freud and forbidden knowledge,* ed. Peter Rudnytsky and Ellen Handler Spitz, 26–41. New York: New York University Press.

Steiner, Riccardo. 2000. *"It is a new kind of diaspora": Explorations in the sociopolitical and cultural context of psychoanalysis.* London: Karnac Books.

Surprenant, Céline. 2008. *Freud: A guide for the perplexed.* London: Continuum Press.

Von Unwerth, Matthew. 2005. *Freud's requiem: Mourning, memory, and the invisible history of a summer walk.* New York: Riverhead Books.

Weber, Samuel. 2000. *The legend of Freud.* Expanded ed. Stanford, CA: Stanford University Press.

Wollheim, Richard. 1991. *Freud,* 2nd ed. London: Fontana Press.

Young-Bruehl, Elisabeth, and Christine Dunbar. 2009. *One hundred years of psychoanalysis, a timeline: 1900–2000.* Toronto: Caversham Productions.

Index